Traditional Crafts
of Scotland

CHAMBERS GUIDE TO

Traditional Crafts of Scotland

JENNY CARTER and JANET RAE

CHAMBERS

Acknowledgments

It has been a privilege to meet so many men and women who are masters of their profession. We are grateful to them for welcoming us into their place of work, for sharing with us their deep knowledge and wisdom and, above all, for demonstrating their pride in quality craftsmanship.

In addition to the many makers we talked to in our travels around Scotland, we also thank Harry Lindley of Kinloch Anderson for his advice on kiltmaking; Tom Speirs (piper), Bill and Alastair Hardie (fiddlers) and Savourna Stevenson (harpist) for their collective knowledge about the music of Scotland; Fergus Wood, Director of the Scottish Woollen Industry for information on textiles; Elaine Kennedy of Dumfries Museum and Dr Helen Bennett for their advice about handknitting; Stewart Beaty for his words of wisdom about industrial knitwear; John Speirs for his guidance on lacemaking; Jack Howells for his help with conservation; the Highlands and Islands Development Board and the Scottish Development Agency for access to their picture libraries; and the many industrialists who gave so generously of their time and expertise. We must also thank everyone who has helped and encouraged us in the production of this book, especially Thérèse Duriez for her meticulous editing, Bill Rae for his careful checking, and Alastair Fyfe Holmes of Chambers for his enthusiastic support.

© Jenny Carter and Janet Rae 1988

Published by W & R Chambers Ltd Edinburgh, 1988

British Library Cataloguing in Publication Data

Carter, Jenny
   Chambers guide to traditional crafts of Scotland.
   1. Handicraft—Scotland
   I. Title   II. Rae, Janet
   680'.9411   TT61

   ISBN 0-550-20000-2

Produced by Carter Rae Editorial Services
Design and layout by F.M. Artwork and Design
Typeset by Hewer Text Composition Services
Printed by Blackwood Pillans & Wilson Ltd. Edinburgh

Contents

Introduction

It could be said that every country starts its craft heritage from the same base – climate and indigenous materials dictating the development of some skills more than others. The need to find and prepare food, to construct shelter, and to protect the body against icy winds or scorching sun, make demands that have always tested man's ingenuity and manual dexterity. In Scotland, as in other countries, craftsmen also came to have social status in the community. The village blacksmith, for example, not only shod horses, made fire irons and gates: his smithy was also the place at which men gathered to exchange news and opinions; the village forge was as important a local gathering place as the village hostelry. The skills of the village weaver were just as vital to the community as those of the smith. Equally important in early society were skills like coopering, tanning and leather working, potting, thatching, boatbuilding, contructing drystane dykes and stone masonry.

Many of these crafts were practised in rural areas by people who had to learn to turn their hand to any necessary chore. But as society developed and jobs became more specialised, individual practitioners of these crafts turned their attention to perfecting one particular skill. Slowly, the demand for their products changed. The cooper's skills have not always been confined to making whisky barrels: initially he made pails for carrying water, churns for making butter, and kegs for storing and transporting anything from flour to gunpowder. The tanner provided leather for shoes and saddles, bottles and buckets and the drive belts of primitive machinery.

Sadly, some traditional skills have all but vanished. In Scotland it is almost impossible, for example, to find a heather thatcher. Once every Highland crofter made his own creels for carrying peat or fish; now there is no more than a handful of basket makers practising this ancient skill. Embroiderers of the present day – and Scotland has some of the finest to be found anywhere – use all the advanced techniques and design skills available to them, but very few have the time to produce old Ayrshire embroidery. This fine white work with its elaborate cuts and embroidery infills, traditionally used on christening gowns and handkerchiefs, is so time-consuming that often it is now made more for sentiment than for selling.

Some craftsmen have adapted their skills to the demands of contemporary society. The wood and stone carvers and masons, plasterers and stained glass artists, having worked in past centuries alongside the builders and architects, today find a fresh appreciation of their skills in many areas – especially in the field of architectural conservation. Other craftsmen, like the drystane dyker, continue much as before, for no modern techniques or machinery can advance the building and repairing of the thousands of miles of stone walling around the country.

Some images of Scotland have become debased by over-usage or by presenting them in an inappropriate context. It is not surprising that many tourists imagine every Scotsman wears the kilt and plays the bagpipes. The truth, of course, is very different. Nevertheless, the kilt *is* worn in Scotland, more so than in many other countries, where national costume is donned merely for show. Fashioning the kilt and its accoutrements is a skilled occupation and part of the national tradition.

The liveliness of the *ceilidh*, the traditional Gaelic evening of song, story and dance, has always depended greatly on the expertise of the fiddler – and he depends in turn on the man who crafted his instrument. Golf clubs and curling stones, though primitive when these games were first invented were improved by people with craft skills – to the ultimate delight of a grateful world.

Some crafts have become industrialised, but even in an industrial situation they retain a hand-work element. Many craftsmen, working in their own studios, use machinery – even computerised technology – in some of the processes. The machine does not diminish the value of these traditional skills: the craftsmen have simply learnt to adapt to a changing world.

This book is selective rather than comprehensive, the authors have chosen products and skills with which Scotland has a long association. *Traditional Crafts of Scotland* is offered as an appreciation of the age-old skills of the land, the way in which they have changed and survived.

Jenny Carter
and Janet Rae

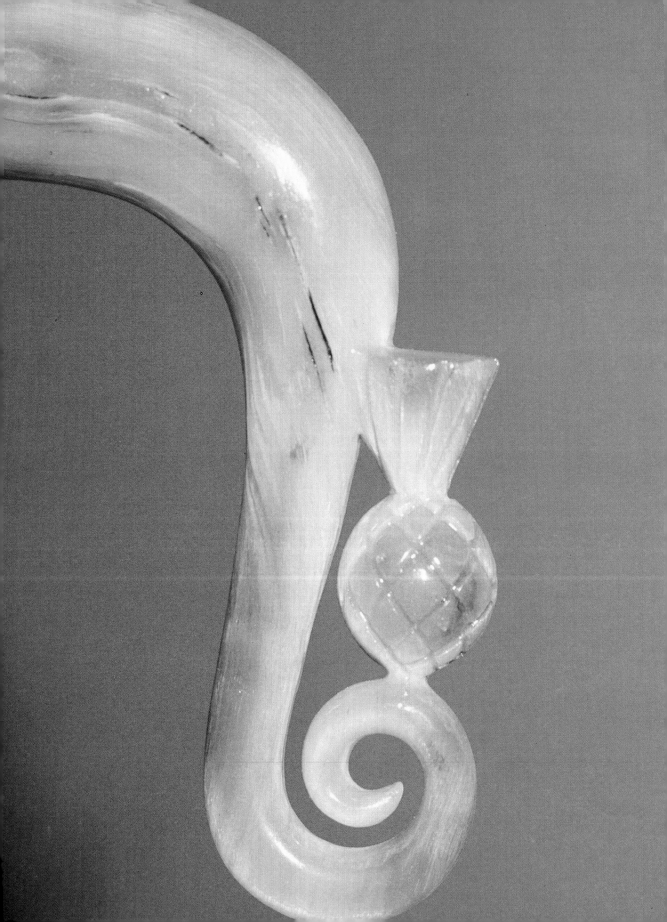

1. Land and Sea

The folk museums of Scotland have many examples of the age-old implements of rural labourers, reminders of days when endless hours of backbreaking toil went into tasks which nowadays are achieved in minutes with modern machinery. We may be thankful for these labour-saving devices but we are also, perversely, nostalgic about the past. Dr Isabel Grant, who spent a life time studying Scottish folk history, was articulate about the attraction:

> More potent still is the actual feel of homely, bygone implements, of stone, metal and wood smoothed and worn by the handling of a sequence of long-dead hands and fashioned by ancient and simple techniques that reveal the individualities of the craftsmen who made them and of the actual pieces of material upon which he worked.[1]

Her collection of such pieces forms the heart of *Am Fasgadh* (the shelter), the Highland Folk Museum at Kingussie south of Inverness. But it is still possible to turn up ancient implements sitting at the back of farm buildings or in the outbuildings of remote crofts. Few people now use a foot plough to turn the soil, but there are many who remember the days when they did.

Dry-stane Dyking

In a society where the successful sale of products or skills is dependent solely on market need, the old rural crafts have been in danger of disappearance. Yet Scotland still has vast areas truly rural in character, where skills like stone walling and the building of boats for local fishermen are much in demand. Thatching has more or less died out as a native craft, but dry-stane dyking has been given new heart by such organisations as the Dry Stone Walling Association, originally formed in the 1960s. The headquarters of the Association is located within the offices of the Young Farmers Club in the National Agricultural Centre at Kenilworth in England, but there are four Scottish branches with a total of about 150 members. The majority of these are sympathetic conservationists and hobbyists – only about 15 work at the craft full time.

Dry-stane dyking began to develop in the Stewartry of Kirkcudbright (now Dumfries

Opposite: Winter's work: a classic shepherd's crook with traditional motif.

(Michael Siebert)

Left: dry-stane dykers at work on the main Carlisle–Edinburgh road at Teindside, near Hawick in 1938. The Elliott family, father, grandfather and son, were among the few craftsmen left at the time who specialised in dyking. The wall, considered to be an 'amenity' was built by the Elliotts in connection with construction of a new road bridge.

(National Museums of Scotland)

and Galloway) about 1710 with the early Enclosure Acts. The type of wall that became commonplace in that part of the country was the double dyke, 4ft 6in (1·372m) high. Here flat stones were laid in level courses and stabilised half way with throughbands (one large, stabilising piece of stone that crossed both walls). The cavity between the walls was carefully packed with small stones and chips. The Galloway walls also had coverbands, that is, stones laid across the top of the dyke beneath the cope. Not all Scottish dry-stane walls had these peculiar design characteristics. The quality, shape and availability of stone within the different regions of the country usually dictated the shape of construction. The north-east of Scotland, with its abundance of granite, produced a style of dry-stane dyke made with large blocks, while in the west, walls were often dyked singly, simply by piling one round boulder on top of another. Whatever the method employed, the skill has always lain in the fitting of the stones. To this day, dry-stane walls are built to last a century without attention. Nor have the tools required for building changed: a 4lb (1·81kg) hammer, a rough wooden frame (batter) to keep the shape

Alan Mackenzie's harness-making workbench on Arran.

(Mike Henderson)

of the dyke uniform during construction, a piece of string and a foot rule are the only implements required.

Harness-making

The collection of horse harness in the Museum at Kingussie recalls the time when horses played a vital role in agriculture and in transport. Rough wooden pack-saddles, placed on top of straw or grass matting to prevent chafing, were used on Highland ponies to carry creels of peat from the upper glens to the croft. Other harness on display emphasises the former value of the horse for ploughing, and for pulling traps and gigs. Scottish harness is distinguishable from English harness in a number of ways, especially in the high peak collars with wide steel hames (tall metal projections which rise from the top of the collar). These high collars are still used for that most popular of Scottish breeds, the Clydesdale. Called the heavy horse of Scotland, the Clydesdale is one breed that has exported well – especially to North America. At home it appears regularly at Scottish agricultural shows, and less frequent-

From plough to parade. A new role for two of the country's most respected working horses.
(Alloa Brewery)

ly in the streets as an eye-catching purveyor of brewery and distillery products. When dressed for show the Clydesdale invariably wears the high Scottish collar, and the harness decoration includes both flowers and brasses.

Harness for both the Clydesdales and other heavy horses is still made in Scotland, but by a diminishing number of craftsmen. Rostie's of Glasgow, established about 1870, is one firm which keeps the tradition of harness-making alive, be it harness for Shetland pony or Clydesdale. However, their fine driving harness and heavy horse harness both reflect the increasing use of horses for sporting events such as driving. Harness once made to pull a plough is now crafted to withstand the rigours of the field trial.

A set of harness has a limited life, and Alan Mackenzie will tell you its manufacture is basically 'strap work'. Mackenzie trained as a saddler at Wainers' College in London and learned the demands of harness-making while working at St Cuthbert's in Edinburgh. He set up as a saddler in Arran in the late seventies

but for economic reasons soon diversified his work to include leather bags and cases.

'The skill in making harness nowadays,' he says, 'lies in making the harness look light and fine for showing. To do this you have to round a lot of the straps so they are not chunky looking.' This is only one way in which the making of harness has changed over the years. Machine-stitching of the leather has generally taken over from hand-stitching. 'Fifty years ago,' says Mackenzie 'the five-foot-long (1·524m) traces that join the horse to the carriage used to have four rows of hand-stitching – 20ft (6·096m) of stitching through half-inch leather. A machine can do this job now in 15 minutes.'

The centre strip of skin in any hide is the toughest and heaviest and it is used for traces and reins where strength is important. The outer parts of the hide, towards the belly, have looser and softer fibres. These are used to make the crupper, the piece of leather which goes under the horse's tail. Choosing tanned hide properly and cutting the straps from the

A selection of work by members of the Scottish Crookmakers Association at the Royal Highland Show.

(Michael Siebert)

correct part of the skin are still fundamental skills of the harness-maker. Not everything has been superseded by machinery.

Crookmaking

The shepherd has been an important figure in the Scottish countryside since the eighteenth century. Until that time, the Highland economy depended largely upon cattle. A few sheep were kept on the crofts for their milk and their wool, which would be spun and used for the making of drugget (dress cloth) or hard-wearing tartan. The large-scale introduction of sheep forced people out of their homes (the notorious 'Highland Clearances') but it introduced a new life into a sector of the economy.

The working of horn – either deer antlers or ram's horn – is one of the most enduring of traditions. Travelling tinkers were among the most skilled of horn-workers, and their spoons, bowls and buttons were familiar everyday objects. Horn was used extensively for the crafting of shepherd's crooks, each maker evolving his own style of product. Fortunately,

this skill has been handed down through members of the Scottish Crookmakers Association. They mount yearly exhibitions, and sometimes demonstrations, at the Royal Highland Show in Edinburgh, where the products of long winter evenings are shown to good effect. This is the one time of the year that the 150 members of the Association sell their work, and the crooks are in great demand. There is an endless variety: tall thumb-sticks, finished with a notched deer antler handle, designed for stalking and the resting of binoculars or a telescope; chest-high crooks which prove of immeasurable support for climbers or shepherds traversing steep slopes; hipbone-high walking-sticks which provide additional support for a gammy leg; and the knob stick which is perhaps more of an affectation than a help.

Hazel, holly, blackthorn and ash are the woods to be preferred for walking-sticks. The handles, sometimes made of wood that has been carved, are more traditionally executed in horn. Curled Blackfaced ram's horn is the favourite for shepherd's crooks but regrettably it is growing scarce. In order to be usable, the horn for a crook must be from a mature ram of five to six years, and nowadays there is a tendency to slaughter rams before the horn has aged to the carver's requirements. As a consequence, the black horn of Indian water buffalo is being used more frequently.

The finished translucent horn handle of a crook – sometimes adorned with a thistle – is achieved by burning, whittling, filing and sanding. Robert Scott, a retired shepherd from Hawick who has been making crooks since he was twelve, starts with a horn that is virtually solid, between 9 and 10in (22·9 and 25·4cm) in length. He applies enough heat with a blow lamp to make the horn pliable and easy to carve with a knife. Additional heat and the use of a vice help to straighten the horn, and the rough material is finished with a rasp. Brasso, or a sand-grit polish, brings out the light beige translucent quality of the horn but if a darker colour is preferred then the horn is coated with a mixture of shellac and oil.

Horn-carvers who work at the craft full time often invent special tools to speed up the traditional process. Leonard Parkin of Newcastletown, Roxburghshire, who started hornwork as a hobby in the late fifties, uses high-speed polishers and sanders and has adapted special cutting machinery, including the conversion of a Singer sewing-machine into a fret saw. He boils horn to assist in the flattening process and makes some 40 different items from both horn and antler. These include the once-popular tumblers, which call for high-quality horn, and take a long time to execute.

Tanning

The tanning of skins is one of the very oldest of crafts; there is evidence that back in the Ice Age the cave dwellers used primitive stone-scrapers to remove the flesh from the skins to make leathers for clothing and footwear. The attraction of leather, despite the advent of cheaper modern synthetic materials, has endured. Leather has an aesthetic appeal – it is also comfortable to wear, softens with age and does not cause perspiration.

In the Ice Age, skins may have been stretched to dry or smoked to provide a rude form of curing. However, skins treated in this way would have soon cracked and become uncomfortable to wear. Natural oils had to be replaced, and fats and brains were rubbed into the skins to achieve suppleness. At some point, it was discovered that the bark of certain trees,

soaked in water, provided a solution – tannin – which gave skins a miraculous sheen and suppleness. The tanning process actually transformed the skin into leather, changing the molecular structure and making a new material. In Britain, oak bark was used because of the abundance of oak trees. Towards the end of the last century, chemicals were discovered which had a similar effect yet allowed the curing process to take place more quickly.

Scotland has a number of tanneries, most of which use the 'chrome-tanning' method involving chromium salts. There still exists, though, at least one small tannery which uses the ancient bark-tanning method. 'Tanning the skins in this way gives them a quality which chrome-tanned skins lose,' maintains Molly Arthur of Grogport Rugs in Argyll. Her speciality is sheepskins, though she has tanned many other skins including deer, leopard, pine marten and fox. 'The back of the skin remains

Molly Arthur processing one of her sheepskin rugs.

(Molly Arthur)

pale brown (hence the term "tanning") instead of turning the characteristic white or blue associated with chemical tanning methods. And not only does the skin remain soft and supple, it can even be washed without losing its original characteristics.'

Mrs Arthur uses powdered bark from Africa (becoming increasingly difficult and expensive to obtain) which is put into a leaching pit with water. Skins are prepared by scraping off the excess fat with a knife and being washed six times to take out the dirt from the skin and the wool. They are then carefully checked for defects before being immersed in the tannin solution for one to two weeks. The skins require to be handled at least once a day to ensure that tanning takes place evenly. The total process takes about four weeks. Once tanned, the skins are stretched on frames to dry and the fleeces softened manually, rubbed with a stone, and trimmed. Brushing, done by hand, can take a long time if the hair is long.

Boat-building

Chris Dawson (right) and a colleague fit the ribbing on a clinker boat.

(John Charity)

The sea, like the land, has its own special influence on Scotland's native life and craft.

Boat-building is one of country's oldest industries and, though the big ships once launched on the Clyde (in or near Glasgow) belong more or less to memory, there are several small businesses – often operated by one man – that still carry on the tradition of building wooden dinghies. Before the development of fibreglass shells, clinker-built boats were made in abundance. Today, it is the boating traditionalists who seek them out. The clinker-built boat came to Scotland with the Vikings. Its chief characteristic is the overlapping planks which form the shell. The carvel type of boat, which had its origins in the Mediterranean, is different in that the strakes or planks of the shell are laid edge to edge. The other chief difference between the two lies in the assembly: in clinker-built boats, the skin of the boat is made first and the ribs and other reinforcement inserted thereafter. Carvel boats begin with the building of the stem, stern-post, ribs and keel – a framework over which the strakes are laid.

Clinker-built boats, nowadays, are made in lengths up to about 35ft (10·668m), though in the past they were built as large as 80ft (24·384m). A 14ft (4·267m) dinghy made by this method takes builder Chris Dawson about a month to complete. Chris, who lives and works by Garve in Wester Ross, is an engineer whose own love of sailing channelled him

towards boat-building. He is particularly appreciative of the dinghy's special qualities: 'Clinker-built boats are heavier, more stable (than fibreglass) and the fish can't hear you so well!' Durability also features prominently in his list of advantages. One of the dinghies in use is over 100 years old.

One of the present uses for these small dinghies is rowing on lochs for pleasure or for angling. But the clinker-built boat is so versatile that it can be built for use with motor or sail and in different weights, depending on how hard a life the boat is expected to lead. 'As long as people don't treat their boats badly,' says Dawson 'they will last a lifetime.' Dawson also repairs boats and one habit which he tries to instil is the storage of these vessels on blocks. 'Too many people leave their boats lying on grass and it rots the timbers,' he says.

Scottish larch is the traditional timber for the clinker-built boat and the keel, stern and ribs are usually made of oak. The difficulty in obtaining mature larch has forced many a small boat-builder to abandon this old craft. Attempts to substitute European Larch with Japanese Larch have generally proved unsuccessful – it is a hybrid timber and lasts only about 15 years.

Chris Dawson uses larch from an estate near Inverness and oak from the Scottish lowlands. And he follows the time-honoured methods of building. First, the back bone of the boat is built; the stem-post, stern-post and transom are bolted to the keel. Next, he constructs the skin of the boat, by overlapping the planks of larch and fastening them with nails. This step, called 'clenching', turns the nails into rivets. The most difficult part of the construction, he says, is building the boat in such a way that the joints between the planks do not leak. The larch itself does not bend into shape without help. Each plank must be steamed in either a box or 'sleeve', then clamped in position until the wood cools and nailing and clenching can begin. After all the shaped planks have been nailed in place, the ribs, gunwale, rowlocks and seats are fitted. No real caulking is required on the clinker-built boats because of their construction. In the old days, the boats were often finished with a mixture of boiled resin and linseed oil and, sometimes, tar. Nowadays, they are generally painted.

Creels

Although the clinker-boat tradition carries on, other crafts once associated with the sea have

disappeared or changed in character. The once vital skill of twisting rope (for land or sea) – from root fibres or heather or rushes or horsehair – is no longer practicable, although the technique of twisting is still used sometimes with man-made fibres. But the making of creels for fishing has become very much a success story in Stornoway on the Isle of Lewis. Island Fabrications, started by Stewart Graham in 1983, currently make 1600 creels a week for the fishing industry. This award-winning venture, which started as a one-man business, now employs 45 full-time workers in a new specially-built factory.

Creels were once handmade of wood or cane, covered with fibre net. Nowadays, the creels made by Graham's company (they market specialist creels for lobsters, prawns, brown or velvet crabs and whelks) are machine-made – a steel frame with a PVC coating – and then manually fitted with the plastic netting and a netting needle. The technique may have been modernised but handwork remains a requisite.

New demand for an old craft: a creel made by Island Fabrications of Stornoway.

1. I. F. Grant, *Highland Folk Ways*, London, 1961, p. xi.

2. In the Home

Domestic furnishings in eighteenth-century rural Scotland were not spartan, but neither were they elaborate. This description of the contents of a Cromarty farm kitchen of 1795 lists the basic essentials: . . . a bedstead, press, meal-chest, clothes chest, 3 chairs, 3 stools, 2 spinning wheels, a reel, 4 wooden dishes, 4 cogs, 3 pots (different sizes), a pan, 10 horn spoons, tongs, a crook or chain for the fire-place, a table, 8 blankets, and 3 rugs or coverings.[1]

At the same time, the Georgian houses in Edinburgh's New Town were well under construction. The first houses to be built in Charlotte Square, in 1792, had at least twelve rooms. The contents of these spacious rooms, with their marble fire-places and ornamental plaster-work, would have been considerably more refined than those used by the Cromarty family in the farm cottage described above. Furniture used by crofters was functional, often home-made and quickly constructed. A 'Sutherland' chair in the collection of the Highland Folk Museum at Kingussie demonstrates the simplicity which characterised

these pieces: a roughly-hewn wooden framework, made of random woods like hawthorn and pine, is linked at the back with spindles.

There were, of course, also a number of fine cabinetmakers in Scotland in the eighteenth and nineteenth centuries, many of whom were influenced by the work of their counterparts in London. A few distinctly 'Scottish' furnishings were created, however, including the 'Scotch' chest, a chest of drawers with a deep central drawer for storing hats (this rather top-heavy piece of furniture was usually made in pine) and the 'Scotch chair' – a mass-produced yoke-backed chair with a wooden seat that appears today in antique auctions.

The Outer Isles had a number of indigenous items, the most characteristic being the box-bed and the long wooden settle. In the Black Houses of Lewis these were lined against the walls alongside a dresser with a plate-rack, a cupboard and probably a chest to store clothes. The arrangement of these simple furnishings was important – space had to be left around the fire, which always occupied the centre of the floor. Although Scotland still

Opposite: Michael O'Donnell, Caithness, turning one of his porcelain-thin bowls.

(Glyn Satterley)

Below: working in a time-honoured tradition – nineteenth-century makers of the Orkney chair.

(National Museums of Scotland)

*Robert Towers of Kirkwall in
his present-day workshop.*
(Robert Towers)

worked in a diversity of widths to be sent to London for making up into bonnets. At the peak of its popularity, straw-plaiting gave employment to 7000 women, earning them an estimated £30,000 annually.[2]

The oat-straw used for Orkney chairs is best when thickly sown and harvested early. It has to be cut either by hand or with a binder, since combine harvesting would damage the stalks. The straw is initially stripped of all its loose stuff or 'slochs'. Then, coils are prepared with the help of a brass ring to ensure an even thickness and sewn together and laced to holes in wooden uprights of the chair. The original binding material for this process was a strong grass called 'bent' but makers today use sisal, which they work with a sack-needle.

The best-known form of the Orkney chair is the one with the hood – originally designed to keep draughts from the head and shoulders. But high-backed chairs, without the hood, and in both adult and child-size, are in the same tradition. In its earlier form, the Orkney chair was made entirely of straw, its base resembling an upturned basket. In the latter part of the nineteenth century, however, a wooden frame was evolved for the chair and in some instances the chairs were also made with a drawer beneath the seat.

Today, the Orkney chair has achieved a loftier status. Instead of being crafted for the humble cottage, it is now often sought by interior designers or collectors in search of an unusual focal point in a room. D. M. Kirkness of Kirkwall was the man responsible for turning this vernacular piece of island furniture into a local industry in the 1890s. He died about 1936, and the outbreak of war in 1939 stopped further production. The revival of this craft began in the 1950s and today one of its chief practitioners is Robert Towers of Kirkwall, who produces both the hooded and straight-backed styles of the chair in pine and walnut, following the very labour-intensive methods employed in the past. Locally-grown oat-straw is used for the backs of the chairs and woven sea-grass for the seats. The technique of using coils of straw secured with a binding is also still used to make baskets – 'cubbies' – on Orkney. Elsewhere, the once common practice of making baskets from grasses, willow or brushwoods has sadly declined. At one time a wide range of baskets was made. One kind was

> . . . used for serving potatoes, with perhaps a relish of herrings. The potatoes were tipped into it from the cooking pot and the water they had been boiled in was allowed to run

has a number of furniture-makers producing hand crafted pieces, it is to the Isles that we must look today for a continuing Scottish *tradition* in furniture – specifically to Orkney, where the distinctive hooded wood and straw Orkney chairs are still being made.

Straw was a very important material to the Orcadians. In earlier times the bleakness of their island left them without more sturdy building components. Historically the islanders proved ingenious in their use of straw: they used straw for thatching, and for making kitchen receptacles for holding meal, eggs and salt. Straw also played a role in working the land and harvesting the sea. It was used to make ropes, tethers and harness; creels for carrying peat; and larger baskets to place across horses' backs. During the eighteenth century there was even a flourishing industry in straw-plaiting: rye-straw was

Harvesting willow for baskets with the help of a friend.

(John Charity)

on to a bundle of fodder, which served as a nourishing bite for any cow that needed special attention. The dish was put on a stool, and the company helped themselves out of it.[3]

Baskets had other functions, too. Wickerwork was used for coffins, for gates and fences, and for furniture – an old larder on display in the Highland Folk Museum has wicker sides. Fisherfolk used baskets to hold bait and to land fish, while crofters used baskets for seed potatoes and pairs of baskets (panniers) to sling over the backs of ponies. Until the 1950s, baskets for carrying peat from the moors were still made by most crofters; nowadays a car will be driven to the nearest point and the peats loaded into the boot. Peat creels were made upside down by planting willow rods into the ground, then weaving thinner switches through them. The framework was gradually drawn inwards, then the ends bound together to form the bottom of the creel and the frame removed from the ground.

Despite a great revival in basket-making in other countries – particularly in North America – there are very few basket-makers left today in Scotland. Perhaps the main reason can be found in the comments of Duncan Mackenzie from Loch Broom, a crofter who still cuts his own willows and makes log baskets and gardening baskets, first weaving the handle and frame and then slowly building on. He uses green willow and will take about seven hours to make one basket, in a process he describes as 'very hard work – work which is tough on the hands'.

Duncan Mackenzie of Loch Broom, one of Scotland's few remaining basket-makers.
(John Charity)

Spinning-wheels

In contrast to the virtually redundant craft of making baskets, the crafting of spinning-wheels is once again capturing the imagination of woodworking specialists. This renaissance of a once-familiar and vitally important piece of furniture has resulted from renewed interest in one of the oldest of the textile crafts – one so rudimentary that its place in both croft and town house was taken for granted.

Social distinctions in old spinning-wheels can be easily discerned: the more elegant, decorated wheels were usually made for the drawingroom and rather genteel use by the lady of the house, who usually spun flax. Below stairs, the spinning-wheel would have been more utilitarian – maids would have worked the wheel for spinning wool.

There are a number of variations on the spinning-wheel, and both the National Museums of Scotland in Edinburgh and the

Highland Folk Museum in Kingussie have many examples. Flax was an important Scottish crop by the eighteenth century and spinning was actively encouraged in many parts of the country. In the Highlands, free wheels were often issued as part of training given in special spinning schools. The wheels used most frequently in Scotland fell into two categories: the 'horizontal', where the flyer was positioned at the side, and the 'vertical', where the flyer lay directly above. Today, this smaller vertical wheel is often called the Shetland or 'Island wheel' because of its former popularity in the isles. John Burra, of Comrie, Perthshire, who makes about 30 of these traditional Island wheels a year, is convinced that the popularity of the design lay in the wheel's weight and portability. 'Spinning bees for single girls who were working to fill their bottom drawer were very popular in Shetland. This is the only type of wheel which would have been light enough to carry in one hand over a rough track for up to 5 miles [8·045km].' A retired forester and keen woodworker, John turned his hand to spinning-wheels when he 'hung up his axe'! The traditional Shetland wheels that he makes are done in mahogany and weigh about 10lb (4·54kg). The design is the result of his own personal research on some 40 Shetland wheels, and he has improved on some of these by providing a wider choice of tension.

Haldanes of Gateside in Fife, specialists in wood-turning, make both vertical and horizontal wheels in beech, as well as small spinning accessories like carders. They turned to making spinning-wheels in 1969 and now export to America, Germany and Japan. The traditional wheels that they make – 'The Orkney' and 'The Lewis' – have been given modern modifications where necessary: ball-bearings have been inserted in the hub of the wheels, for example, to make for smoother spinning.

Damask

The revival of interest in spinning has centred on wool and the use of hand-spun yarns for knitwear rather than the spinning of flax, which was once an essential part of Scotland's important linen industry. The growing of flax was well established in Scotland by the mid-1600s, and at that time flax was spun on a spindle not a wheel. Woven linen had innumerable uses in the seventeenth and eighteenth centuries, not only shirts and undergarments but all manner of household needs and also

sail-cloth. Linen weaving was especially encouraged in Ireland and Scotland, where public funding was available to all branches of the industry and where Boards of Trustees were established in the mid-1700s to set standards of quality and uniform lengths and widths. In Angus, where a heavier or coarser grade of linen was woven for sail-cloth, some landowners allocated specific land feus to weavers to grow flax and for bleaching greens as well as for houses which would include workshop space for looms.

The art of weaving was revolutionised by the French inventor, Joseph Marie Jacquard, who invented a loom capable of producing woven designs. First introduced in Paris in 1801, by the mid-1800s, damask weaving on Jacquard looms had developed as another important branch of the linen industry in Scotland. In Dunfermline they were used in the 1820s for damask weaving, and in Paisley for the coveted Paisley shawls. The looms were also used in Angus and Kincardineshire, the other main weaving centres. It is this speciality of the once-flourishing linen industry that remains today in Scotland in the person of Ian Dale of Angus Handloom Weavers who has a workshop at House of Dun by Montrose, south of Aberdeen.

Ian Dale was initiated into weaving as a boy in Luthermuir when he earned pocket-money by helping William Taylor, a local craftsman. It was not until the late 1970s, however, and only after a number of years working as an engineer, that Dale returned to Luthermuir to rejoin the then semi-retired weaver. Dale is now the only weaver of hand-loomed linen damask cloth left, and he works on 100-year-old Jacquard-looms. On a good day he can weave 9yds (8·23m) of 20in (50·8cm) cloth, hand-throwing his flying shuttle 78 to 80 shots per inch of damask.

The Jacquards are complicated looms which rely on intricate punch-cards for their patterns and also call for some stamina: Dale sometimes works for ten or eleven hours at a stretch. Reloading a loom with a new warp can take him as long as 100 hours, since the loom must be virtually dismantled before it can be rewarped with 60 to 100yds (54·86 – 91·44m) of flax, at the rate of 80 threads to an inch of warp. The Jacquards were originally used to weave silk and Dale hopes to reintroduce the weaving of this luxury fabric on one of his four Jacquards. In the meantime, however, he weaves a few traditional damask designs such as thistles, wild roses, and Celtic and geometrical patterns. Most of these are woven in

Above: punched cards are used to determine the design in the Jacquard loom. On a good day Ian Dale can weave 9 yds of patterned damask.

Right: the classic appeal of handwoven linen damask.

white on white – a combination which has found favour with generations of housewives who prize the pristine appearance of a well-laundered and immaculately-ironed linen table-cloth or towel. But Dale also weaves in blue, gold, green and pink and will do specialist orders incorporating family monograms or initials. He can weave cloths up to 90in (2·286m) in width.

During the summer months, Dale gives regular demonstrations of damask weaving at the Angus Folk Museum in Glamis near Dundee. And nowadays he can boast that he uses Angus-grown flax instead of the French flax which he used when he resumed his weaving career in the seventies. Flax is being grown again in Scotland (albeit on a small scale) thanks to the encouragement given to farmers by the Scottish Development Agency.

The method of turning flax into linen fibre is complicated, however, and as yet no mechanised process for this is available in Scotland. Dale keeps between 15 and 20 tons (15·24 and 20·32 tonnes) of flax in storage but sends it to Belgium for scutching (the process used for removing the broken straw) and to Ireland for wet spinning.

Wood-turning

Many traditional Scottish cookery and eating utensils were once crafted by tinkers – the 'travelling people'. Their repertoire included horn spoons, baskets, brushes and pot-scrubbers, and silver and tin smithing.

The making of horn spoons was one craft in particular that the travelling people guarded closely, and until the mid-nineteenth century, these spoons were widely used. The small 'leppel' and the larger 'gibbie' horn spoons are still made in the traditional way, by heating the horn and pressing it into a spoon mould. Unfortunately, the heat of modern dish-washers can ruin these traditional eating implements as they need special care in cleaning.

Other old and familiar cookery utensils – especially those made of iron – are now found only in antique shops. The bannock spade, that heart-shaped turning implement which came in so many different variations, the iron oatcake toaster which hooked on the edge of the fire-place grate, and the iron 'brander' or split girdle for baking oatcakes and bannocks over the open fire, have become items of curiosity rather than usefulness. Women today can still make their traditional pancakes and scones on a round girdle but if they buy it new, it is more likely to be cast steel than iron and designed specifically for gas and electric cookers instead of an open fire.

Wood, however, continues to have a place in the crafting of household ware, and Scotland, like most other countries, still utilises the talents of the wood-turner. Perhaps the most distinctive and enduring ethnic bowl produced by the country's wood craftsmen was the quaich, a shallow cup with a handle on either side. The early examples of this cup were carved from solid pieces of wood, but by the seventeenth century the more elegant versions were being turned on lathes, the base being finished with a silver-coin inlay.

The quaich has been crafted in various materials – including horn – and by various methods. At one time many were made on coopering principles, bound together by the hoops-and-staves technique employed in the manufacture of casks. 'Coggies' (large wooden buckets) and 'luggies' (beakers with a handle), were also made by this method. In Orkney the tradition of the 'Bride's Cog' still remains. It is a large wooden drinking-vessel with two or three turned handles projecting from the rim, and it, too, is built along coopering principles – with brass strips replacing the traditional

Today's turned bowls, while functional, also have a fine decorative quality. Turners like Iain McGregor use the innate properties of the wood to best advantage.

(Della Matheson)

willow hoops. The cog has a meaningful role in wedding celebrations:

> all recipes for the filling have one thing in common: they are lethal if you are inclined to over-indulge . . . The first drink is taken by the bride, then the groom, the bridesmaid, and the best man, then the guests. But always the cog should go round the hall in the direction of the sun.[4]

Nowadays, the quaich has moved distinctly up-market and is usually produced in silver as a presentation or christening gift. Turned bowls of the functional type, however, have been made and utilised for centuries and today this tradition is carried on in Scotland by such makers as Iona and Iain McGregor, whose workshop is situated at the Homestead Craft Centre within The Hirsel estate at Coldstream in the Borders. But like the silver quaich, bowls made by these craftsmen are greatly superior to the functional vessels made in centuries past. Although they remain functional they are also highly decorative and sit easily in an art gallery atmosphere.

Modern practitioners of wood-turning have added a new dimension to this traditional craft. Both the McGregors and wood-turners like Liz and Michael O'Donnell from Thurso, are enthusiastic about the possibilities of using green wood, as opposed to seasoned wood, because of the distorted shapes that can be produced. The O'Donnells, who work with Scottish hardwoods like laburnum, burr elm, holly and sycamore, are also noted for their fine, as opposed to chunky, turning. Their bowls are thin enough to let light through and can have the appearance of fine porcelain. They are often carved and decoratively painted.

The McGregors, using locally grown cherry, beech, oak and ash, produce bowls from 8 to 44in (20·3cm–1·118m) in diameter and none is duplicated. Their work begins with the purchase of a suitable tree, which is marked and cut with a chain saw. Bowls are turned on a lathe while still green, and then kiln-dried for six to eight weeks down to an eight per cent moisture content. Iain McGregor, who does all of the lathe work, likes chunky turning and feels that the misshapen forms which often result from the kiln-drying have a pleasant tactile quality. His wife Iona, who is in charge of the finishing, uses a special slow-turning sanding-machine to compensate for the dis-

Turning sycamore.

(Michael Siebert)

tortions in the irregularly-shaped bowls. She finishes each bowl with three coats of non-toxic, lead-free oil.

A very different style of wood-turning can be found in the work of Stanley Whyte of Pathhead, Midlothian, who left his family grocery business in 1968 to work with wood. His work is perhaps best known in association with traditional baking. In a good year Whyte will, single-handed, turn as many as 9000 shortbread and butter moulds. Each has the traditional thistle emblem carved in the centre. He also makes spurtles with a thistle head, the

stick used through the ages for stirring porridge.

Almost all of Whyte's moulds are made of locally-grown sycamore, a wood chosen because it has no taste and is odourless. Whyte also buys whole trees: a good one will yield as many as 200 moulds. After cutting the tree into sections on a band-saw, he roughs out the mould on a lathe. The carving of the thistle and the chipped border pattern is done by hand and the moulds are finished by sanding. It is left to the cook to oil the wood in preparation for baking shortbread.

Moulds for traditional shortbread 'rounds': prolific wood-turning by Stanley Whyte of Pathhead.

(Michael Siebert)

Above: the castle is Edinburgh's Hallmark symbol.

(National Museums of Scotland)

Below: silver coffee pot by Adrian Hope, purchased by the National Museums of Scotland.

Silver

In the more sophisticated Scottish households, silver played an important part, reaching its peak of popularity, perhaps, in the eighteenth century. Then every household aspiring to fashionable taste would have at least a tea-pot of fine quality.

The fashioning of silver is an ancient craft. In 1483 the Edinburgh Guild of Hammermen (goldsmiths) were granted a Seal of Cause in acknowledgement of their ability to be self-regulating, while records of the establishment of standards date back earlier, to 1457, 'anent the reformation of gold and silver wrocht be Goldsmithes, and to eschew the deceiving done to the kingis lieges.'[5] Because silver and gold must be worked as alloys (mixed with base metals) standards of purity are necessary to establish value. The method of registering this standard is the 'hallmark' which, from 1681 in Edinburgh bears the maker's mark and the town mark (the castle), a date letter and the mark of the Incorporation's assay-master. Glasgow was much later to add the date mark (1819), and other Scottish cities used it hardly at all. By 1836 all Scottish work could be assayed only in Edinburgh or Glasgow, and in 1963 Glasgow's assay office closed. All silver and gold made throughout Britain can now be marked only in Edinburgh, London or Birmingham.

The English influence in terms of taste could not be avoided, especially after the Treaty of Union of 1707, when many of the Scottish aristocracy also had homes in London. Nevertheless, Scotland has always had distinctive tastes in the matter of silver ware, with a preference – perhaps in accordance with the national character – for strong, plain lines, without an excess of ornamentation. Pieces which were distinctively Scottish include thistle cups which were used for wine and were made in the late seventeenth and early eighteenth centuries. These are now very rare. Bannock-racks, made to hold the big flat oatcakes, are also extremely rare. Fish-slices of the late eighteenth or nineteenth century, however, may still be found; these were a popular item among silversmiths, as the large flat blades gave much scope for ornament.

Tea arrived in Scotland in the eighteenth century; a Scot, William Mackintosh of Borlum, recorded in 1729 that 'in lieu of the big quaigh with strong ale and toast and after a dram of good wholesome Scots spirits, there is now the tea-kettle put on the fire, and silver and china equipage brought in with the marmalet, cream and cold tea.'[6] Scottish tea-pots were large and spherical with a slightly flattened top and base. The lid continued the line, while the handles were elegantly curved, and the spout emerged from low on the body. Milk jugs and sugar bowls in matching shapes were also popular between 1720 and 1750. Spoons have always had an attraction (and even with today's prices for new silver are still collectable), while the crumb-scoop was a distinctively Scottish item. This curved piece of silver on a handle, made from about 1760 to

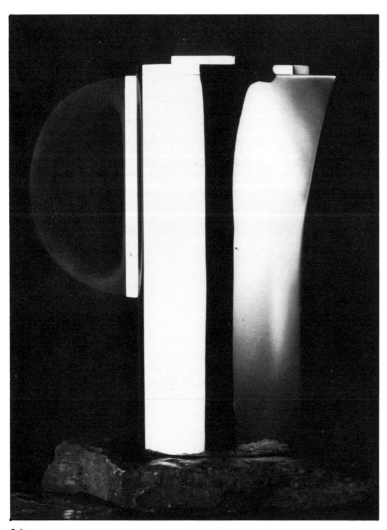

1820, was used to sweep across the table to gather up the crumbs.

Trencher salts took over from the central salt-box of medieval days by the seventeenth century; sets of four, six or more were placed round the table. Sugar casters came into fashion after trade with the West Indies brought sugar and spices to the country, and from the late seventeenth century it was common to have three or more sets. Mazers were once a popular form of drinking vessel, and were originally fashioned from wood. Wealthier households added silver decoration, and gradually goldsmiths adopted the shape as their own. Tumblers – again distinctively Scottish – were so called because of their rounded bases, which allowed the cup to roll or 'tumble' back upright if they were knocked. Porringers were bowls from which soft food was eaten – not just porridge – and quaichs, originally simple wooden vessels, achieved a popularity as silver items from the seventeenth century. For some reason quaichs have become the most enduring of distinctively Scottish silver, and are still widely made in the country, not for their traditional use as drinking vessels, but largely for gifts or presenta-

tions.

Goldsmithing was not something that was easily entered into; an apprentice had to serve for seven years, then one year as a journeyman (if he was a burgess's son) or two years if he was a 'stranger' and he had to have £500 in goods or land (a considerable wealth), as well as pay a fee to the Incorporation. Finally, the applicant was given an 'essay', usually two pieces which had to be made in a workshop under the eye of two masters. Many essay-pieces have survived, and are of great interest. Smithing often ran in the family, and famous Scots goldsmiths included the Coks, the Heriots (the famous Jinglin' Geordie Heriot endowed a school which is still one of Edinburgh's most famous schools), the Craufords and the Kers. Less well known is Ebenezer Oliphant, the smith responsible for the magnificent travelling canteen which belonged to Prince Charles Edward Stuart (Bonnie Prince Charlie). The silver-gilt canteen made in 1740–41, consists of a set of travelling cutlery – two tumblers, two forks, two spoons, a teaspoon/marrow scoop, a nutmeg grater/cork-screw and a cruet. The canteen was lost after the battle of Culloden and fell into the

Nowadays quaichs like these by T. K. Ebbutt are more often made in silver than wood and are used for presentations.

(Michael Siebert)

hands of the Duke of Cumberland, who presented it to the Duke of Albemarle. In 1963 it was sold to a collector; it came up for sale again in 1984, when it was purchased by the National Museums of Scotland in Edinburgh after a campaign to raise the purchase price.

The skills of the silversmith have never been lost, and Scotland still trains many fine workers, though now more in the art colleges than through the traditional apprenticeship system. The 1950s saw a peak in the commissioning of church silver, but financial problems and the closure of many churches have meant that little new work has been commissioned, while older plate has been sold or gifted to other churches. The Incorporation of Goldsmiths of Edinburgh itself suffered a crisis in 1979, when there were only four masters. An application for a revision of the Charter was successful, and ensured the future of the Incorporation.

Several Scottish smiths have received important commissions; John Creed of Glasgow crafted a ciborium for the Pope's visit to Scotland in 1982, a jewel casket for the Scottish Crafts Collection, and a set of goblets to mark the 300th anniversary of the Incorporation of Goldsmiths of Edinburgh in 1987. Jon Hunt, a young smith who qualified in England and now works in Edinburgh, was commissioned by the Incorporation to make a liqueur decanter and twelve noggins for presentation to the Dublin Incorporation in 1987. Malcolm Appleby of Crathes, one of the finest engravers in Britain, has worked on many important items, and a coffee-pot by Adrian Hope of Edinburgh was purchased by the National Museums of Scotland as a fine example 'in the tradition of Scottish silversmithing'.

'It is impossible to be a smith and *not* work in the tradition,' says Hope.

New techniques are really just an extension of the old ones. Nowadays, we have the benefit of very sophisticated refining processes which provide us with metal which is much more easily workable. We have accurate solders and good fluxes; and we have the advantage of motor-driven machinery, gas torches, ultrasonic cleaning processes and automated methods of polishing. Nevertheless, these are peripheral – a sixteenth-century smith walking into my workshop would recognise all the essential tools and equipment.

The joy of working with silver is that it is so forgiving. You and the metal can really work together, and you don't need elaborate tools. Many tools are home made. Any procedure requiring expensive machinery can be sent out. Many silversmiths, for example, will subcontract spinning or even raising, simply making sure that the design is good and the brief exact.

According to Hope, the vogue for commissioning silver for the domestic table has returned. 'I find that many people simply can't find what they want in the shops. They don't want reproductions, they aren't interested in the small amount of Scandinavian work they can find, and they are prepared to seek out a silversmith who can produce something special.'

Many silver companies still operate on a more broadly commercial basis, producing production lines of spoons and small items in traditional style. The acquisition and collection of smaller items of fine Scottish silver thus remains within the pocket of many.

Clocks

Clocks were not often found in Scottish homes until the eighteenth century, and even then only in the more affluent households. Public clocks, on the other hand, were known in some Scottish communities as early as the fourteenth century and the profession of clockmaking was well established by the beginning of the seventeenth century.

There are two traditional types of clock, the bracket clock, meant to stand on a table, and the long-case clock. The mechanism of the former is driven by a coiled spring, while the latter works by a system of descending weights.

The quaich: polishing is an important step.

(Michael Siebert)

Patience and precision workmanship are the key qualities for clock mechanisms – especially for regulators. Every component in this brass escapement by Timothy Brameld was made at his workbench.

29

More long-case clocks were made in Britain than anywhere in the world, and Scottish retailers of clocks would often put their names on clocks which had English mechanisms. The cases were made in oak, mahogany or walnut veneer and sometimes decorated with marquetry (inlay of different coloured woods). By the mid eighteenth century, artists were being employed to paint scenic or figurative pictures on the dials. Fife people, for example, liked pictures of ships and fishing boats on their clock faces – a reminder, perhaps, of the fact that many depended on the sea for their livelihood.

The challenge of making unusual time-pieces is one Scottish tradition that has survived over the centuries. John Smith of Pittenweem in Fife (1770–1814) was perhaps the most remarkable practitioner of the musical clock. The description of his masterpiece is perhaps slightly embellished with the years: an eight-day long-case clock, 7ft (2·134m) tall with three dial plates and sixteen chime bells. The clock had a repertoire of eight different Scots reels, including 'Roslin Castle' and 'Highland Laddie', and it played a different tune every three hours – the tempo of the music could even be changed to triple time. As each tune played, it set in motion a procession of fifteen Lords of Council and Session preceded by their macer. The clock itself showed the hour, minute and second, also the day of the month and the day of the week, Sunday being observed by the casting up of a special note on the dial, 'Remember Sunday'. This clock is believed to be one of the two musical clocks by Smith in the collection of the National Museums of Scotland, Queen Street, Edinburgh. Other examples of his work can be found in the Chambers Street premises of the National Museums in Edinburgh and in Kirkcaldy Museum and Art Gallery in Fife.

Smith made other remarkable clocks and his achievement is all the more noteworthy, given his rural situation and his lack of contact with others in the same profession. Eighteenth-century Dutch trade with the East Neuk of Fife may have influenced his work. Certainly he was not in the happy position of a present-day Fife clockmaker, Alan Hamshere, who has, on occasion, researched old clocks in London's Guildhall.

Alan Hamshere, in many ways, maintains Smith's affinity for the unusual timepiece – in present-day terms, the 'feature clock'. He has created a number along traditional lines but is working towards a more complex clock which would feature automata:

Public clocks could be far more decorative. Generally they are bland though functional. With intricate mathematical calculation and precise engineering it is not impossible to make an impressive and decorative clock which would attract attention more readily than a purely functional one and hence become a feature within or without a building.

One of Hamshere's largest commissions to date – a clock with a face measuring 5½ft (1·676m) in diameter – is sited in the new Britoil offices in Glasgow. The clock, which is both astronomical and astrological and goes for one year on a single winding, registers a number of facts: high tide at Dundee, Glasgow, Aberdeen and Leith; sunrise, sunset, moonrise and moonset in Glasgow; the hour in 24 different locations throughout the world; the day and month of the year; signs of the zodiac, and so on. What it does not register is time to the second – that, says Hamshere, is what people wear wrist-watches for.

Clockmaking as a craft has changed in the twentieth century. The precision engineering of individual parts is both time-consuming and expensive, and hand-made clocks usually are not undertaken unless by commission. Consequently, present-day clockmakers supplement their earnings with repair work. Hamshere especially likes the challenge of repairing big clocks – the challenge that may begin with the discovery of a mechanism 'buried under a mound of pigeon droppings'. One clock that he first viewed in this state, 82ft (25m) above ground level, has now been restored to working order. It is sited in a turret on a private development near Perth. Hamshere believes there is a resurgence of interest in such clocks but he would like to see an increased awareness, on the part of the public, of the maintenance required to keep these public time-keepers in good order.

Timothy Brameld of Edinburgh is another craftsman captivated by horology (the science of time measurement). He is particularly interested in precision time-keepers which over the years have come to be known as regulators. Regulators have traditionally been used to set other clocks by, and their history goes back to the seventeenth century.

The role of precision mechanical time-keepers cannot be overstressed; without them, much of what we take for granted today, like a single time standard and the marine chronometer, would not have been possible. The first practical solution to the problem of accurate time-keeping was made by the Dutch scientist,

Christian Huyghens, who in 1657 devised a mechanism that maintained the motion of a pendulum. During the following 50 years others made individual contributions to the development of accurate time-keeping including Thomas Tompion and George Graham, who are the only clockmakers to be buried in Westminster Abbey. It is the fascination of making a mechanism able to keep time to better than one second per week that interests Tim Brameld, although he points out that the ability of his regulators to keep time is no better than many made in the eighteenth century – despite the improvement of tools. His own well-equipped workshop, where a wheel cutting engine, or a lathe can be set in motion at the touch of a button, is a sharp contrast to the rudimentary tools used by clockmakers of old. Brameld even uses a personal computer to calculate the dimensions of certain components, prior to machining.

His commissions include a numbered edition of ten gravity-escapement regulator clocks cased in mahogany and polished lacquered brass. The clock workings, known as the four-legged gravity escapement, are based on a principle invented by Lord Grimthorpe, who designed Big Ben for the Palace of Westminster. The pendulum, which beats

seconds, is a large, mercury-filled glass jar mounted in a stirrup. It swings by the weight of two arms which fall alternately on either side of the pendulum rod. The weight is a polished brass cylinder.

His most ambitious project has been the design and construction of an astronomical clock which would achieve the same accuracy as a simple regulator. As well as telling time, the clock displays the phase of the moon, the relative positions of the planet Jupiter's four innermost moons, the time of sunrise and sunset, the equation of time – the difference between solar time and mean time – and the day, date and month on a calendar that takes into account leap year.

1. Sir John Sinclair, *General View of the Agriculture of the Northern Counties and Islands of Scotland*, 1975, p. 77.
2. John Firth, *Reminiscences of an Orkney Parish*, Stromness, 1974, p. 49.
3. I. F. Grant, *Highland Folk Ways*, London, 1961, p. 188.
4. Robert Towers, 'Here Comes the Bride's Cog' in *Woodworker*, April 1980, p. 246.
5. Donald Wintersgill, *Scottish Antiques*, Edinburgh, 1977, p. 19.
6. *Ibid.*, p. 20.

The clockmaker's workshop of today is equipped with both traditional tools and modern technology.

(Michael Siebert)

3. Keeping Warm

The bride she cam' out o' the byre, an' O as
 she dichted her cheeks,
'Sirs, I'm tae be married the nicht an' hae
 neither blankets nor sheets;
Ha'e neither blankets nor sheets, nor scarce
 a coverlet too:
The bride that has a' thing tae borrow has
 e'en richt muckle ado.'[1]

Spinning

This tale of the Orkney lass improvident
enough to wed before she had mastered the art
of spinning and had woven enough blankets
for her dowry, recalls the time when every item
of bedding and clothing was hand-produced.
Spinning was the necessary step between the
fleece and the loom or needle, its place in the
domestic order as important as cooking or
growing food.

The spindle-whorl preceded the wheel.
The spindle itself, likely made of wood, came
in a number of varieties. The whorl, a stone
with a hole, was used to provide additional
weight and increase the impetus of the spinning. The spindle was highly portable and,
unlike the wheel which followed, could be
used by the spinner as she walked to market or
herded the cattle. In the Highlands, spindle-
whorls were also considered to be charms. Dr
Grant, author of *Highland Folk Ways*[2] owned
two made of deer's antlers, which allegedly
had been placed in the thatch above a cottage
door by a witch.

Spinning as a source of employment, and
the use of the spinning-wheel, grew alongside
the flourishing linen industry in the eighteenth
century. Hand-spun and woven linen sheets
were commonplace – even in the remote parts
of the Highlands – and rough linen shirts were
commonly worn by the working classes. Linen
was not, as it is today, considered a luxury
fibre. The spinning of wool for blankets and
woollen clothing also featured in the spinner's
repertoire, as did dyeing with native plants like
oak bark, nettles and heather. Wool was
usually dyed after it was spun and washed but
before it was woven, since most spinners had
no large pots or vats, and were required to
work with small quantities. Often the dyeing
took place out-of-doors, the dyeing pot being
filled with layers of the plant to be used and
mordants to combine and fix the dyes. (As well

as plants, peat soot was also used if a yellow-
brown colour was required.) The pot was
boiled and stirred over an open fire, and the
results were often very uneven.

The importance of the spinning-wheel as a
source of income declined with increasing
use of mechanisation in the textile industry.
Today, it has reappeared in a limited way as
a cottage industry and as a focus for home-
knitters who wish to follow traditional methods
of yarn preparation.

The Silverbirch Workshop at Whiting Bay
on the Isle of Arran is one cottage industry
which has managed to keep spinning viable.
But much of its success can be attributed to the
particular characteristics of an island eco-

*Opposite: the much coveted
Harris Tweed woven by
Marion Campbell has a
hand-spun weft and is
coloured with natural dyes in
the traditional way.*

(Glyn Satterley)

*Below: it takes Debbie Gray of
Muthill 20 to 30 hours to
handspin enough wool for one
sweater.*

nomy. Most of the fleeces used for spinning come from island sheep, and the ten or so women employed as spinning outworkers look upon the reward for their work as a good supplementary income, not a living wage. Additionally there is the bonus of tourism – the workshop offers summer courses and maintains a lively profile through constant contact with spinners abroad.

Silverbirch was started in the mid-1970s by Lynn Ross, and even then she viewed her enterprise as comparable to the co-operative economic logic which sustains countries in the Third World. She uses island produce and island labour and has somehow managed to keep her prices stable despite inflation elsewhere. And she has won the ear of the local farmers, who seek her view on breeding sheep as well as the importance of unmarked fleeces: putting a keil or red marks of identification on the backs of the sheep ruins the fleece and is becoming an obsolete practice.

The spinners at Silverbirch originally used the wool of the island's Blackface sheep but now prefer fleece from a crossbreed between the Blackface and the Blue Leicester. The chief attraction of this wool is that no carding is required before it is spun: the wool possesses the best qualities of the two breeds – softness and a long fibre. Most of their spinning is in two-ply, but the Silverbirch spinners also do the very fine single-ply Shetland wool that is used for lace knitting and silk and wool mixtures. Half of what they spin is exported, to the Continent and North America, the trade having developed simply by word of mouth. They use plants from the surrounding countryside, such as heather and birch leaves, for dyeing the wool, and when developing a new fibre mixture always test the wool by knitting up garments. Their experimentation with spinning has also included the growing and processing of flax by traditional methods.

Another spinner who works professionally is Debbie Gray of Muthill in Perthshire. She uses fleeces from a number of different breeds including the Cheviots and Cheviot crosses, the Black Welsh Mountain, Shetland and even Scottish Mohair goats. She also spins silk and linen and mixtures. Most of Debbie's output – and she estimates it takes 20 to 30 hours to spin enough wool for an adult-size sweater – is left in its natural state and sold after washing. She has, however, done some successful experiments in rainbow dyeing – dyeing the fleeces before spinning.

Fleeces usually are delivered to a spinner direct from shearing, without any intermediary cleaning. They can weigh anywhere from 2½ to 15lb (1·135–6·8kg), depending on the breed, and usually require a bit of handpicking to clean off stray bits of brush and dirt. Debbie's first step, after cleaning, is grading: the back of the neck and shoulders of the fleece provide the softest wool, while the back is used for medium quality yarn and the hind legs for rug yarn. Nothing is wasted – fleece from the tail and belly go into the compost pile or into fertilising the potato crop.

The natural grease in a fleece is important to successful spinning and this is the chief reason why washing of the yarn is done when the spinning is completed. (In Orkney, additional grease – a mixture of whale-oil and tar – called 'creesh', used to be sprinkled on the wool to make it more pliant before spinning: the rancid smell was ultimately washed out of the cloth with strong soap and soda.) The wool itself, when undyed, can show pleasing blends of natural colours of greys and whites and beiges. The fleece providing the best black, in natural form, is the Black Welsh Mountain sheep but even here there can be slight variations: a fleece that has been bleached in the sun and then spun without carding will produce yarn featuring specks of browny-orange.

Weaving

Hand-weaving has as much of a tradition in Scotland as hand-spinning, and before the making of tweed was introduced into the Highlands in the mid-nineteenth century, there were a number of woven textiles ranging in quality from coarse to fine – the finest, of course, being linen. Blankets, hard-wearing woollen serge and twill, 'drugget' and 'cloutie' all figured in the work of the local weaver, who was often also a farmer. The spinner, having completed her hours of work at the wheel, would take him her yarn for weaving into the cloth of her choice. In Orkney there was a 'warping boonta' (bounty). The housewife, when delivering her yarn, also took the weaver a cheese and half a stone (3·18kg) of meal, which she handed over once the warp threads were on the loom but before the weaving had begun.[2]

The weaver's work was hard and he was ill-paid, considering the importance of his role. Certainly he was versatile: drugget (*drogad*), for example, was a cloth originally made with a linen warp and a woollen weft (later the warp was changed to cotton) and usually dyed dark blue. Women used it to make rough working skirts and until recently its production had virtually died out. One couple, Tom and Lesley Kilbryde who live near Shieldaig in Wester Ross on the north-west coast, have revived an interest in the cloth and now weave it in their croft. 'Cloutie' was the special province of weavers who had passed their prime and it was rough in appearance: it had a weft of thin strips of old stuff (containing worsted yarns) woven on a cotton warp, and was used for quilts. Blankets were also woven – white 'Ayrshire' blankets with an indigo stripe around the outside and a coarse and heavy 'goose-eye' pattern, usually woven at 28in (71·1cm) wide and then roughly seamed. The weaving of plaiding was also a Shetland speciality for centuries (it died out as a home industry in the mid-1800s) and rent was often paid in plaid cloth.

The high value placed on woven cloth and knitwear through the years – especially in the Outer Islands – is best demonstrated in the registered trade-names. The 'Made in Shetland' label may only be applied to a garment if it really has been made in the Shetland Islands, while 'Harris Tweed' has to be made in the Western Hebrides, using Scottish wool. Tweed itself originated in the Borders although it was originally called *tweel*. (The popularity of Sir Walter Scott and his romantic novels about the Border country, plus a clerk's misreading of handwriting, was responsible for changing the original name of the textile.) Tweed became a mechanised textile in the Borders in about 1820. It was a coarse woollen stuff in natural colours of white, grey and black and its development as a home industry in Harris is attributable to the efforts of one woman, Lady Dunmore, wife of the island's owner.

The first half of the nineteenth century was a difficult period in the Western Highlands and Islands. Bad fishing seasons and changes in old styles of agriculture made the introduction of new industries desirable. Some lairds and their ladies set about introducing handcrafts to their tenants as a possible source of income: in Gairloch on the north-west coast, Lady MacKenzie successfully introduced the knitting of stockings; in Harris, Lord Dunmore had his family tartan (Murray) woven in the local plaiding for wear by himself and his gamekeepers and other employees. It was Lady Dunmore, however, who introduced the weaving of tweed to the islanders about 1850 and then set about marketing it among her wealthy friends in London and the south.

The hard-wearing properties of tweed have always made it eminently appropriate for country pursuits. Its up-market quality image, originally projected by Lady Dunmore, has continued to this day. Added to that is its association – especially for the American, European, and latterly Japanese markets – with romantic and distant islands. The appeal of tweed on these counts seems universal. The success of the cloth has inevitably meant the introduction of some degree of mechanisation in the manufacturing process. A semi-automatic treadle-loom was introduced into the making of tweed in Harris in the 1920s and from the mid-1930s the dyeing, spinning and finishing processes were handed over by the crofters to small mills based mostly in Lewis. At present 750 weavers – all self-employed – work in the islands, and the tweed they produce generates an annual turnover of £35,000,000.

Despite the size of its annual turnover, tweed remains essentially a cottage industry in that nearly all the weaving is still done in the homes of the crofters – albeit on mechanised treadle-looms. About ten weavers still use the old flying-shuttle looms, but almost all use the island mills for their supply of wool and for the heavy finishing process.

Marion Campbell, now in her late seventies, still undertakes most of the work in the traditional way. Her wool comes from the adjoining croft and is coloured with natural dyes from the local lichens, 'yellow flowers', iris roots (which yield yellows and brown), or with chemical dyes for the greens and blues. The combed-out wool is sent to Lewis, where the warp threads are spun to give them greater strength, while wool for the weft is sent back to Miss Campbell to spin – 'to give the cloth greater softness.'

Miss Campbell is one of the few weavers who uses an old flying-shuttle loom: hers was acquired by a sister in 1919. The foot-pedal operation is strenuous; so, too, is the next process, the 'waulking' of the cloth to make it shrink and firm up. At this point it reduces from the 31in width (78·7cm) at which it is woven, to 29in (73·7cm), the standard width for Harris Tweed.

The 'waulking o' the wab' was once observed as a great social occasion. Once the cloth had been cut from the loom, eight or ten local women would congregate around an old table, or a door that had been laid across two stools, and begin working the cloth by pulling, rubbing and twisting. This always had to be done in a circular motion that followed the path of the sun. The new web, which had been

soaking in an ammonia solution, was usually placed hot on the improvised table and the women sang as they worked and generally engaged in good-natured cameraderie:

> While passing the wisps of claith round the board, one considered it quite a good joke to give his neighbour a slap in the face with a fold of it, or, better still, to put a twist of it round his neck. The fun sometimes became so furious that the end of the web would be thrown over a paun-tree, much to the detriment of the cloth.[3]

Regrettably there are few left now to remember the social custom of waulking. Marion Campbell is one: 'In my young days we used to travel from croft to croft in groups of five or six. We always sang the old songs while we worked. Now I'm the only one doing it.'

The finishing of Harris Tweed is essentially unchanged. Once it has been shrunk, it is pegged out to dry – the windy Hebridean climate being more suitable for this purpose than hot sunshine since it makes the cloth softer. The finished cloth is then rolled and stored, or parcelled and despatched to fulfil orders.

Harris Tweed is not the only survivor of a once prolific hand-weaving tradition. Rugs, shawls, scarves, suitings and tapestry are still made by a number of independent, self-employed weavers: Veronica Togneri of Inverness-shire, who designs floor and travel rugs; Kirsty McFarlane of Lanarkshire, who specialises in double-face weaves for domestic use; and Water Lily Weavers of Roxburghshire, whose woven wall-hangings reflect the Scottish landscape. Some weavers, like Russell Gurney of Aberdeenshire, supplement the produce of their looms with tuition; others like Hugh Gray of Perthshire take their weaving a step further by making up the cloth into clothing. Gray's very distinctive patterns – 'rosepath', 'barleycorn', 'goose-eye' and 'herring bone' – all executed in colours that suggest the Scottish landscape, are made into capes and jackets. Some of Scotland's weavers have organised themselves into a marketing co-operative. The North of Scotland Hand-loom Weavers' Association, for example, has a membership drawn from north of an Oban (on the west coast)/Arbroath (on the east coast) axis (including the islands). Their collective strength and strategy make the penetration of certain sales markets more feasible. Other weavers continue to weave and sell on an individual basis, carrying on the tradition of a cottage craft.

Knitwear
Ganseys

Scottish knitwear is so often identified with women and rural industry that it is hard to believe it originated in anything other than the land and a need to keep warm. This is one of many misconceptions that have grown with the development of this most prolific of all Scottish crafts. As Helen Bennett points out in her book, *Scottish Knitting*, 'The earliest knitters in Scotland were not women knitting for their families but craftsmen working in Lowland towns. These professional knitters, called bonnet-makers, are first heard of in the fifteenth century.'[4]

Bonnet-makers made small, flat, woollen caps and stockings and gloves. They were numerous and professional enough to have their own trade guilds. A few even managed to make a comfortable living from this traditional item of headgear. The bonnet had certain properties suitable to the Scottish climate: knitted in rough wool and then shrunk to tighten the stitches, it was virtually waterproof.

Another common misunderstanding about traditional (as opposed to contemporary Scottish knitwear) concerns the Aran pattern – the heavily patterned cream sweater worn by fishermen. Many visitors seeking out this particular garment assume it originated in the Isle of Arran off the west coast of Scotland, when in fact its origins are in the Aran Isles off Galway Bay, Ireland. Seekers of ethnic Scottish knitwear should really concentrate on Shetland, Fair Isle, Sanquhar and Eriskay knitting as samples of the country's true indigenous patterns. The first two have enjoyed a long and commercial prosperity, while the third – Sanquhar – is barely known outside Scotland. The Eriskay jersey, which is firmly in the country's gansey (fishermen's jersey) tradition, has more of a domestic than a commercial heritage.

One of the best places to study the importance of knitwear to past generations of fishing folk is the Fisheries Museum at Anstruther on the Fife coast. It is believed that fishermen's knitting reached its peak alongside the development of the herring industry in the nineteenth and early twentieth centuries. Men would leave their home ports for months at a time to fish off Shetland and the Hebrides in the summer and East Anglia in the late autumn. They went with their kists (chests) full of home-knitted garments: each would have five or six pairs of long drawers (knitted in a pinkish colour called 'Shetland grey' and

Opposite: Hugh Gray of Perthshire weaving his distinctive multi-coloured cloth.

The crew of the Violet *during a call to Oban in 1935. The navy gansey was a necessary garment in the fisherman's kist.*

(Fisheries Museum, Anstruther)

made up with a cotton waistband and cotton-lined crotch-gusset), five or six pairs of sea-boot stockings (which fit over the trouser leg up to the knee), shorter working stockings, mittens, scarves and five or six of the all-important gansey, the distinctive patterned jersey which was almost wind and watertight.

Considering the contents of these kists, it is no wonder that the fishing womenfolk carried their knitting in their apron pockets and took out the needles at every opportune moment. Women played a very important role in the herring industry and not only as knitters. The herring girls who followed the fleets from port to port had the very arduous task of gutting and packing the fish in barrels. Working at speed, a group of two gutters and a packer could clean and grade as many as 70 herring a minute. To protect their hands, many wore crude cotton bandages wrapped round their fingers, which they slipped off, in the odd moment, in order to take out the knitting. Injuries were frequent and the life hard.

Herring girls knitted ganseys and other garments, not for sale but for the menfolk in the community, and unlike other distinctive patterns to be found in Scottish knitting – like Fair Isle – the gansey never became 'fashionable'. For this reason it is still not a sweater than can be easily purchased over the counter. Co-Chomunn Eirisgeidh Ltd, on the Isle of Eriskay, is a co-operative which continues the gansey knitting tradition in an industrious, but

limited way. The small population of this island, which lies between Barra and South Uist in the Outer Hebrides, means there are few women left with time to invest in this labour-intensive task. The co-operative has only ten knitters and in a year they can hand-knit only 50 jerseys. Such is the continuing popularity of the gansey, however, that their order books are always full.

Ganseys have a number of distinguishing characteristics. First, they are always knitted in navy or cream wool. The Eriskay knitters used five-ply wool (which is now becoming a difficult ply to find) and four British size-ten, steel needles. Ganseys are always knitted in the round (without side seams) and because of this they are easy to repair. There is no sewing on these jerseys (even the sleeves are knitted from stitches picked up at the armhole), and worn-out necks, cuffs and even whole sleeves can be renewed with comparative ease by unravelling the worn bits, picking up the stitches and reworking. Sleeves were, in fact, often knitted slightly shorter than required since no fisherman wanted or needed a wet cuff wrapped around his wrist. The only other stylistic feature was the high neck and the figure-hugging shape of the gansey.

The colour of the gansey is traditional – in some British sea ports the cream gansey was reputed to be used as a wedding shirt. The colour navy had a practical side because it was not discoloured by sea-water. The ply of yarn and the closeness of knit gave the gansey its wind and waterproof qualities and made it a standard uniform among working fishermen. The other single distinction of the gansey was its patterns. Although some fishermen preferred plain garments, others liked the many different stitch patterns which their womenfolk created and knitted into the ganseys. At one time, it is said, it was even possible to identify the home port of a dead sailor by the design on the gansey he wore. Women based their designs not only on the elements but also on certain symbols of the fishing industry. The moss-and-rope pattern was used often as were diamonds. There was even a Scottish-flag or 'kilt-pleat' pattern.

Many ganseys have patterns only on the sleeves and chest. The Eriskay gansey has always been distinguished by its overall patterns. The logo of the Eriksay co-operative is a

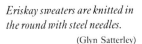

Eriskay sweaters are knitted in the round with steel needles.
(Glyn Satterley)

flower – the flower that tradition says was planted on Eriskay by Bonnie Prince Charlie when he landed on the island to begin his ill-fated attempt to win the British crown. The patterns used in the Eriskay jerseys, however, are closely allied to the island's fishing economy: the starfish, harbour steps, the anchor, fish-net, cable and wave. Each of the knitters in the co-operative knits a collection of these traditional motifs in whatever fashion she chooses, thus giving each jersey its own distinctive style.

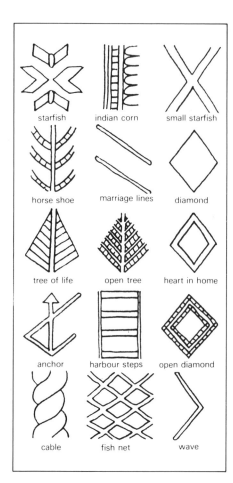

Sanquhar Knitting

Right: Eriskay sweaters made by the island's co-operative knitting group use many traditional patterns.

(Co-Chomunn Eirisgeidh Ltd)

Below: the Sanquhar patterns require the skills of the more advanced handknitters.

(Dumfries Museum)

Another type of Scottish knitting, labour-intensive and not often found for sale, originated about 200 years ago in a small town in Dumfriesshire. Sanquhar knitting is a distinctive chequer pattern used chiefly in gloves although originally it appeared in stockings. Keen knitters seeking a challenge are responsible for keeping the Sanquhar tradition alive today, as is the Scottish Women's Rural Institute. The SWRI has taken the trouble to

publish patterns and to set occasional Sanquhar knitting exercises for members. Examples of this knitting, indigenous to south-west Scotland, can be seen at Dumfries Museum.

Sanquhar knitting is done in two sharply contrasting colours, such as black and white, and it is believed to have originated in the eighteenth century when the town had both an abundance of sheep and a number of woollen manufacturers. The favourite (perhaps because it is the easiest) Sanquhar pattern today is the Duke Design, made in three-ply wool on British size-16 needles. (The size 16 is used for lady's size, while size 13 or 14 are used for men's gloves.) The gloves, made with the knitter holding the black wool in the right hand and the white wool over the first finger of the left hand in Continental fashion, have another distinguishing design feature: initials are knitted into the inside wrist of the gloves – a practice at least 100 years old. Other traditional patterns also appear in Sanquhar: the 'Shepherd's Plaid', the 'Prince of Wales' and the 'Midge and Fly'. All have their own distinctive charm: none can be said to be suitable for a novice knitter.

Shetland/Fair Isle

Shetland knitwear is a generic term which today covers lace, plain and the two-colour pattern knitting known as Fair Isle. Any item of knitwear which bears the logo of the Shetland Knitwear Trades Association – the picture of a lady knitting – guarantees that the item has been made on the islands by one of the 2000 people who work in the industry, either full or part-time. More than half a million garments a year are produced in Shetland, either by hand-knitters, or on hand-frame or power-frame machines.

Knitting has been established in the Shetlands for centuries. Traditionally it supplemented the household's income from crofting and fishing. Hand-knitted caps, gloves and stockings made by island women were bartered with European traders until at least the early nineteenth century, when frame-made hosiery made their work redundant. It was then that the women were encouraged to try their hand at knitted lace. Lace of all types was

a fashionable commodity at the time, and the use of wool for the delicate open patterns proved an almost instant success. The Island of Unst, the most northern island in Shetland, in particular developed a reputation for christening robes, shawls and stoles. As the technique grew in popularity, however, lace knitting was also used for spensers (ladies' vests), cardigans, jumpers and even curtains. Lace stockings were presented to Queen Victoria and the Duchess of Kent in 1837, and in 1851 a Shetland lace wedding-veil was displayed at the Great Exhibition.

It is believed that many of the patterns used in traditional Shetland lace have Spanish origins, although a number of patterns used over the years bear such everyday names as spider's web, cockleshell, fir tree and waves. Fine Shetland lace shawls (sometimes called cobweb-lace) are made from the softest part of a fleece – the throat – which is spun into a single-ply yarn. The most treasured shawls, perhaps measuring 5 or 6ft square (1·524 or 1·829m), are those which are fine enough to be

Traditional lace shawls being finished by washing and stretching on frames.

(Shetland Museum)

drawn through a wedding-ring and which weigh less than 2oz (56·7g). The intricate knitting skills required by the makers of these gossamer-like pieces must be matched by equal care in finishing: although lace shawls were once pegged out to dry after washing and bleaching, they are usually washed and stretched on a frame.

Shetland lace fell out of fashion at the end of the Victorian era – especially when it was made to compete with the machine lace made in Nottingham. It is still made today – but often by machine. The number of hand-knitters who will undertake this very time-consuming and special type of work, is dwindling.

Gema Ord of Yell, Shetland, is one hand-knitter who carries on the Shetland lace tradition. She has, however, devised her own method of creating the cobweb lace christening shawls and capes and the slightly heavier two-ply ladies' shawls. Instead of knitting on two needles, and then seaming, in traditional fashion, she uses circular needles and simulates seams by decreasing stitches.

It takes Gema Ord about six weeks to make a shawl, from initial design stages through finishing. She uses many old patterns in her work – horseshoe, Shetland fern and 'print of the wave' – and she says that patience and concentration are prime requisites for lace work. Unlike many knitters who can happily work and talk at the same time, she requires peace and quiet.

Traditional Fair Isle patterns are usually knitted in the round. Why this complex pattern

Above: contemporary Shetland handknitter.

(Gunnie Moberg)

Right: the annual Royal Highland Show is a regular venue for displaying the variety of Scottish fleeces.

(Michael Siebert)

ever developed on such a remote and sparsely populated island is mainly conjecture: one popular theory is that the patterns were taught to the islanders by shipwrecked Spaniards from the Armada of 1588. Another theory says the patterns reached the island via Russian and Scandinavian traders. Whatever the origin, the Fair Isle sweater did not achieve popularity until the 1920s, when Edward, Prince of Wales, was photographed wearing a Fair Isle jumper with an all-over pattern.

Fair Isle patterns are usually knitted in colours – only two being used at a time. Another kind of pattern knitting, which also originated in the Shetlands, traditionally uses natural coloured whites, creams and fawns, contrasting with dark shades. The heritage of these unique designs is seen today not only in the many different examples of knitwear made in the islands, but also in the work of native Shetlanders who have carried their skills elsewhere. Betty Addison, for example, who took her own bit of Shetland to Edinburgh

many years ago, remembers learning to knit at the age of five. 'There were so many of us in the family that we weren't allowed to use steel needles in case we poked each other's eyes, so we practised knitting with matchsticks. The trouble was, that if you knitted too tight, the heads rubbed together and lit.'

Like other hand-knitters who have used their skills for a lifetime, Betty Addison knits more by instinct than direction. 'I just start with the first row and then I know where I am going.' Patterns are all in her head – never on paper and there is a certain disdain for the plain knit jumper – 'it's all too easy!'

1. John Firth, *Reminiscences of an Orkney Parish*, Stromness, 1974, p. 39.
2. I. F. Grant, *Highland Folk Ways*, London, 1961, p. 223.
3. Firth, *op. cit.*, p. 46.
4. Helen Bennett, *Scottish Knitting*, Aylesbury, 1986, p. 3.

Many of the traditional patterns used in Shetland knitting are believed to have been influenced by European traders.

(Shetland Knitwear Trades Association)

4. Highland Dress

Tartan

Scotland and tartan, tartan and Scotland – in the popular mind the image and the land are equated. But how much is mere myth?

The clan system with which tartans are associated was very much a Highland phenomenon. It related to a belief in a common ancestry, to a leader or chief who was held in respect as the 'father' of the clan, with all followers as equals and brothers. The chiefs established their precedence over a long period of time and usually by right of the possession of land. Most clansmen following a chief resided on his land, so that in addition to a blood tie there was also a sense of community – although as many chiefs held lands in different parts of the country, it was not unusual for clansmen to be widely scattered.

The clan system predominated in the Highlands for about six hundred years, from the twelfth to the eighteenth centuries. It was also a period that saw the Lordship of the Isles emerge as a dominant force in much of the north and west of Scotland, the Hebrides (except Bute and Arran), Kintyre, Lochaber and Morven.

The Lordship proved a powerful guardian of Gaelic culture as well as a political force, and many carved standing-stones of Celtic interlaced and complex design – which still provide a source of inspiration for craftsmen today – date from this period.

The clan system itself disintegrated after the second Jacobite Rising in 1745. At the time of Culloden, 26 chiefs were able to call out nearly 19,000 men. The cost of the Rising in real terms was enormous; many chiefs had their lands annexed and themselves fled to France or elsewhere. Those who remained faced an enormous burden of debt. No longer could they support the old clan system. Yet the old loyalties never truly died away, and the interest in clans and tartans throughout the world today is one of the most remarkable of social phenomena.

The connection between tartan and the clan system is not entirely clear. It is certain that Highlanders wore checked coloured cloth – possibly woven in this fashion because it was easier to make up cloth using a selection of colours rather than dyeing large pieces of cloth a single shade. The complex structure of the tartan cloth may also relate to the Celtic love of intricate patterns: '. . . the complex, stylized designs of the tartan have the same feeling as one finds in Celtic art – the interlaced patterns, the complex verse forms and the construction of the *piobaireachd* [pibroch].'[1] There would naturally be a tendency for local weavers to develop their own styles and colourways, and thus would have developed patterns with district associations. This held true for Lowland checks and for the stripe and colour combination in simple shawls woven in the Outer Isles as much as for the conventional 'tartan'. One observer, travelling through the islands towards the end of the seventeenth century, wrote:

> The Plad, worn only by the men, is made of fine wool, the thred as fine as can be made of that kind; it consists of divers colours, so as to be agreeable to the nicest fancy. For this reason the women are at great pains, first to give an exact pattern of the Plad upon a piece of wood, having the number of every thred of the stripe on it. The length of it is commonly seven double ells . . . Every Isle differes from each other in their fancy of making Plads as to the stripes in breadth and colours. The humour is as different thro the main land of the Highlands, in so far that they who have seen those places are able at the first view of a man's Plad, to guess the place of his residence.[2]

There is evidence to show that the close family of some of the chiefs began to wear tartan of similar colourways by the end of the eighteenth century and the beginning of the nineteenth, although there is no evidence that use of a *clan* tartan was widespread. Perhaps the single most important factor in the preservation and development of the use of tartan as a 'uniform' and as a distinguishing feature was the formation of the Highland regiments in the eighteenth century, and particularly after the '45.

The English government, quick to see the potential of the fiercesome Highlanders as fighting troops, began to rechannel loyalties into a wider British context. Schooled in warfare, and with little in the way of employment at home, Highlanders began to enlist for service, often overseas. The Highland Regiments were exempt from the Disarming Act

Opposite: Harry Lindley, a director of the old Edinburgh kiltmaking firm Kinloch Anderson, displays a length of tartan for making a single kilt.

(Michael Siebert)

The 12th Earl of Eglinton, painted by Copley, shows one of the many ways in which the kilt has been worn.

(National Galleries of Scotland)

which banned the wearing of tartan and, effectively, the playing of the bagpipes (see page 64), and their adoption of regimental tartans and continued playing of the pipes were critical in the preservation of the old traditions. The Act was repealed in 1782, largely because of the Highlanders' magnificent contribution to the war effort in the American War of Independence.

From that time, the wearing of tartan was patchy. In some areas it had always been worn, despite the Disarming Act. An important element in the reviving of its popularity was the formation of the Highland Societies in London (1778) and Edinburgh (1780). These societies, formed to promote Highland culture, did much to popularise the bagpipe and the kilt. The wearing of Highland dress was encouraged, too, by the work of Sir Walter Scott as tourist officer extraordinary. Scott, determined to promote Scotland's beauties and further its standing in the world, laboured to publicise its attractions. Crucial in gaining the attention and respect of the English was the visit to Edinburgh in 1822 of George IV. The King appeared in Highland dress at a levee held at Holyroodhouse on 17 August – the traditional outfit supplemented by a pair of flesh-coloured clinging pantaloons. He disliked the flapping of the tassels on the sporran, and developed a new style, flattened and pinned down.

The King was not alone in wearing the kilt; George had commanded all his loyal chiefs to attend him in Edinburgh wearing their Highland dress – the so-called 'Tartan Review'. The order threw most of these gentlemen into considerable confusion, used as they were to following English fashions. Indeed, recollections of family tartans were largely vague, and many chiefs turned to Wilson's of Bannockburn, near Stirling, or similar weaving companies to construct or reconstruct the old patterns. Weaving by this time had moved from the hands of local weavers into larger, professional concerns, both to cope with demand and because the introduction of sheep-farming made woollen weaving possible on a large scale. Weavers such as Wilson's began to catalogue their designs in pattern books, often labelling setts merely by the use of numbers. The weaving demanded great expertise in the setting up of the intricate warp.

Following George's visit and the birth of a new romanticism about the Highlands, several of the chiefs had their portraits painted in full Highland garb by the renowned portrait painter, Raeburn. The 'Tartan Review' was mas-

sively influential in the revival of popularity in the wearing of tartan. Wilson's experienced a boom in business, installed power weaving, and saw huge new areas of trade opening up in Europe and in America.

The growth in the tartan industry since that time has been immense. In 1831 one list of tartans catalogued 55; in 1961 I. F. Grant mentions a figure of 'around four hundred'.[3] In 1987 the Scottish Tartan Society claimed to have on record over 2000 researched and authenticated tartans. Almost all tartan weaving today is undertaken in the big mills of the Borders, where huge quantities of cloth are produced to satisfy world demand. Not all tartans are recorded officially at the office of the Lord Lyon King of Arms in Edinburgh, but many are recognised through long use as being 'authentic'.

The strength of tartan is its flexibility – far from being confined in a rigid tradition, new setts are constantly being designed. The age-old Black Watch tartan was made in the familiar dark shades of black and green to suit the night watchmen who wore it when on guard against cattle thieving. Today's designers will accommodate other requirements; they may have little need to design for camouflage, but they will pick up colours from armorial bearings, for example, or from company liveries. When British Gas Scotland had a tartan designed to commemorate the great Scottish pioneer of gas, William Murdoch, it picked out shades of the well-known 'British Gas blue'. The tartan is now used by the British Gas Caledonian Pipe Band. Other tartans have been designed for specific occasions – the 1986 Commonwealth Games, for example. And recently two important Lowland families decided that the time had come to research and establish their ancient lineage with the Lord Lyon. Once the line and the chiefship had been officially established for the Agnews and the Moffats, armorial bearings were drawn up and registered, and a suitable tartan for Lowland chiefs was designed (in this case by Mr Lindley at Kinloch Anderson) and also recorded.

Few weavers still produce tartan hand-looms. James Scarlett of Moy near Inverness is one craftsman who has spent a great deal of time researching tartans, and still enjoys producing yardage by hand to order. The cloth produced is equal in quality to tartan woven on power-driven looms; the advantage is simply that it is easy to produce smaller quantities. Scarlett has produced one length of tartan for the Culloden Visitor Centre, built on the battlefield where the Jacobite troops were defeated by the Hanoverians. Appropriately, the tartan is a reproduction of a scrap of material found on the scene of slaughter.

Kiltmaking

The kilt – one of the most complex articles of clothing that a modern tailor may be asked to make – had simple origins. Originally, the garment consisted of a single piece of cloth, made from two strips of 28in (71·1cm) wide tartan seamed down the centre. It measured between eight and eleven yards in length. The *feileadh mor* (philamore) or 'greater kilt' was always an exclusively male garment.

The vast piece of cloth would be laid on the ground and loosely pleated at one end. The Highlander then sat on the pleated area, gathered it round him and belted it at the waist. The remaining yardage was flung over the shoulder, wrapped securely round on cold days, or arranged round the head as a hood in

wet weather. The versatility of the garment was astonishing. At night the cloth was un-belted and used as a sleeping blanket. In battle, if the need for freedom of movement became paramount, the simple act of unbuckling the belt allowed the entire garment to fall to the ground, from where it could later be recovered – should its owner survive. To the philamore would be added a leather pouch, used for carrying oatmeal or coins or, later, gunpowder.

Throughout the centuries the kilt has adapted itself to current needs. Hanoverian soldiers were exempt from the ban on the wearing of the tartan but for them the wearing of a scarlet coat was mandatory. Thus the huge yardage draped over the top half of the body became superfluous, and was effectively cut off, making what became known as the *filibeg* (philabeg), or 'lesser kilt'. To this might be added a long plaid for dress wear – a throw-back to the old philamore which is still used by present-day pipers. A belted plaid was used by drummers, allowing freedom of movement.

The planning of a kilt is skilled and intricate work.
(Michael Siebert)

'The kilt has evolved as a garment for the people,' says kilt expert Harry Lindley of the old Edinburgh firm of Kinloch Anderson (founded in 1868). 'It is not merely a national garment for show, which happens sometimes in other countries. It has adapted itself to become a truly practical garment. The modern kilt is the most practical version of all.'

The skill of the kiltmaker involves more than sewing together the cloth. The huge length – between 8 and 11yds (7·315 and 10·058m) depending on the size of the man – has to be pleated to look like a plain piece of tartan. The kilt is made with two overlapping aprons of plain tartan in the front, while the material is pleated all round the back to give the same appearance as the plain tartan in front. The 'sett', the pattern repeat, varies from tartan to tartan; the sett on the tartan for a child's kilt may be 3½in (8·89cm), on a woman's 5½in (13·97cm), on a man's 6½in (16·51cm), so folding needs great care and planning. As Mr Lindley says,

The quality of a kilt lies in the depth of the pleat. In addition to matching the pattern, the kilt must follow the contours of the body, so that when it is worn it hangs straight with no sagging at the back. The process involves complex mathematics. We *build* kilts here.

Once pleated, the cloth is hand-sewn, then the extra cloth at the back is cut away. Binding is put on to strengthen the structure, then heavy canvas, and extra strengthening is stitched round areas of strain where the belt and buckle are. The straps are stitched on by hand, and a cream lining and quality buckle are added. The fringing down the front edge is usually double, but can be triple.

A kilt will take upwards of twelve hours to make – 17 for a top quality, hand-sewn garment. An apprentice used to serve five years to learn this complex craft; today's apprentices can pass through in three.

The accessories worn with the kilt are all a throw-back to the original. 'A well-made kilt will need no kiltpin,' says Mr Lindley, 'but in the old days a pin might be worn at the waist – usually of stag horn or wood.'

No stockings would have been worn under the philamore, which was worn down to the ankle and merely hitched up for practical purposes. But walking across rough heather moors with a short kilt was a scratchy business, and the kilt hose began to be favoured. These would not be knitted. They were made from a piece of cloth cut on the bias and seamed up the back. Nor did they necessarily match the tartan of the kilt.

The 'ghillie shoe' was deerskin, gathered in one piece and worn over other shoes, laced with a thong and tied round the ankle. The shoe was 'aerated' – the forerunner of the brogue – to let water out. Otherwise, the shoe might simply fill with water and become saturated.

The belt, originally a key component of the dress, became more or less redundant when

The range of sporrans made at Scott's is wide. The large horsehair sporran (centre) is especially popular with pipe bands.

(Michael Siebert)

the top half of the kilt was cut off. Now, to be correct, it should be worn only over the doublet. The sporran, originally to carry provisions or coins, is still a prominent part of the outfit, and has both a practical and a decorative purpose.

Sporrans

Details of design may have changed over the centuries, but the sporran has remained the same in all essentials. One innovation was the patented 'top-opening' sporran of William E. Scott and Son of Edinburgh, which simplified access.

Scott's have been in business for over 50 years, and despite the increased use of machinery to cut down the monotony of some of the more repetitive tasks, their craft remains largely a hand-skill. 'The sporran will never be

William Scott of Scott's in Edinburgh has been making sporrans for a long time. 'Business,' he says, 'has seen a great upsurge.'
(Michael Siebert)

mass produced,' says William Scott. 'It's not possible to eliminate stages which demand hand-skills.'

A plain sporran will take about an hour and a half to produce, one with Celtic poker work on it much longer. An elaborate dress sporran might take as long as a day and a half.

Many leathers used for sporrans are Scottish – pigskins and cowhide are the most common. Deerskin is not used, as the hair is not well rooted. Other skins used are musquash, morocco, goatskin, mink and pony. Horsehair sporrans are the most popular for pipe bands, as the long hair tassels swish picturesquely with every step.

The horsehair does not come from the knacker's yard. All the hair used is gathered by grooms in studs and racing stables around the country from combings. It is then treated meticulously for anthrax, and finally reaches the sporran-maker's in long tubes. The hair is laid out and arranged into long strips, bound by adhesive or pleated to keep it secure. A horsehair sporran has six layers of hair, from 11 to 17in (27·9–43·2cm) long; arranging the layers will take twelve hours.

The sporran is basically simple – a shape is cut from leather, a gusset sewn round, the front stitched and bound on, and tassels threaded through. Most of the work goes into the decorative aspects, the gathering and sewing of the tassels, or the pleating of the thongs. Some sporrans have elaborate silver or chrome mounts which must be fitted and secured, over a coloured piece of leather which both forms a decorative background and protects the skin when the metal requires cleaning.

The sporran-maker finds demand for his goods higher than it has ever been. 'Business has increased 100 per cent in the last 50 years,' says William Scott. 'The kilt as a garment looks set to remain as popular as ever.'

Putting the finishing touches to a dress sporran.

(Michael Siebert)

Dirks and *sgian-dubhs*

Every Highlander carried arms – a dirk or dagger suspended from his belt, a targe or shield and, if he could afford them, a claymore or 'big sword', a pair of Highland pistols and a gun. These weapons were carried as a matter of course, helping to 'account for their belligerence and pride and also the respect which they paid to each other.'[4]

Contemporary wearers of the Highland dress forego the carrying of powder-horns, targes or pistols, but a few may carry a dirk, and most will wear the *sgian-dubh* (skene-dhu) in the stocking. The dirk is much longer than the *sgian-dubh*, and often incorporates a small fork and knife as well as a large blade. Originally, the handles were heavily carved with intricate Celtic knotwork patterning, acting both as decoration and serving as a firm grip. By Victorian times the pattern had lost its original practical purpose and had assumed a

thistle shape, while other decorative features such as cairngorms began to appear. The dirk had degenerated into an ornament.

Some time in the late eighteenth century, the custom of carrying a *sgian-dubh* seems to have started. The 'black knife' (so called from the colour of the handle) is worn down the stocking, with its decorative setting appearing out from the top.

Today, most jewellers making dirks and *sgian-dubhs* have refined the work to a point where the elements of hand-skills have been reduced to a minimum. The blades, of stainless steel, are imported from Sheffield; the handles, once of ebony and elaborately figured, are now cast in a hardened plastic. It is largely in the decoration that hand-skills are used.

The scabbard is fashioned from boxwood, cut, joined, filed to shape, and covered with Moroccan leather. The decorative mounts are cut from a silver sheet using templates, and bent over by hand to fit the scabbard. Often these mounts are then hand-engraved. The decorative finish on the handles varies in design, but often incorporates a cairngorm or other semi-precious stone, secured by a silver mount pinned through the handle.

Jewellery

Truly traditional Scottish jewellery originally had a purely practical function. The swathe of loose-flowing cloth which was arranged and

Opposite top: the silver mounts for cairngorm stones for the top of sgian dubhs *must be carefully made by hand.*
(Michael Siebert)

Opposite bottom: Neil Ochiltree of T. K. Ebbutt, the Edinburgh-based jewellers, has worked as a silversmith for 45 years.
(Michael Siebert)

Left: a silver plaid brooch with a single cairngorm stone.
(Michael Siebert)

Putting the finishing touches to the brooch.

(Michael Siebert)

draped into garments for both men and women was held together by means of brooches or pins. At their most primitive, these pins would be fashioned from horn or from wood, but early intricately decorated brooches have survived, with copper, silver or gold inlaid decoration in elaborate Celtic tracery. By the Middle Ages, precious stones and pearls were often added, and the Celtic imagery manifested itself through zoomorphic forms chased or engraved on to the metal. By the seventeenth and eighteenth centuries, plaid brooches as large as 8in (20·3cm) in diameter were not uncommon.

While the decline in the weaving of tartans was matched by a decline in jewelled accessories, the Victorians took up the traditional Scottish brooches with enthusiasm, following the lead shown by Queen Victoria when she made Balmoral her Scottish home and insisted

that her young family should be dressed in the kilt. The Victorians, though, added some inventions of their own. A magazine published in 1878 observed that

> The effect of the . . . rich colours of the clan-tartan is enhanced by a multitude of engraved silver buttons, shoulder brooches, embossed buckles, jewelled dirks, etc. until, in a full and archaeologically correct Highland costume – there is a perfectly dazzling combination of silver – burnished, dead and frosted – combined with precious stones.[5]

The display was, of course, anything but 'archaeologically correct': plaid brooches popular in this period were a 'marriage' of earlier forms – the rim of metal with a huge cairngorm in the middle combined the medieval and plaid types. The Victorians embellished and elaborated the traditional forms, adding jewelled thistle shapes and 'lucky claw' brooches by way of making their own stamp on tradition. But the work of Scottish craftsmen during this era was greatly valued (much 'Scottish' jewellery at this time was made in Birmingham, Dublin or Germany) and was shown with pride at international exhibitions of the arts.

Certainly, Scottish jewellers have been fortunate in the abundance of raw materials available to them – silver and gold from Lanarkshire, charming asymmetrical pearls from the River Tay, and pretty agates and pebbles in abundance. The renowned 'Woman of the Stones' who lived near Braemar in Aberdeenshire in the late eighteenth century dreamed one night of a huge cairngorm 'beckoning her from the rocks of Beinn a' Bhuird'.[6] She found in the place of her dreams a crystal that weighed 52lb (23.59kg), which may be seen at Braemar Castle.

The one Lowland form of brooch which became popular and has survived over the years is the 'Luckenbooth' – so called because it was sold from the locked jewellers' booths clustered around St Giles Cathedral in Edinburgh. The heart-shaped brooch was a popular symbol of love, and was given at a betrothal, often engraved with initials or a verse. The brooch was said to be a potent protection against witchcraft, and one eighteenth-century writer observed that girls wore them on the left hip, boys on the left thigh. The more

elaborate versions of the Luckenbooth featured two hearts intertwined, often surmounted by a crown. The 'M' effect created linked the brooch in the popular mind with Mary, Queen of Scots, but the connection is mere romantic fancy.

Today in Scotland the tradition of jewellery-making remains strong. In art colleges students have a high record of achievement in national and international competitions, and many craftsmen make and sell both precious and non-precious jewellery of innovative contemporary design. But the popularity of the traditional styles of jewellery have not faded, and there are many crafts businesses making Celtic-style brooches, thistle brooches with amethysts or cairngorms, Luckenbooths of varied styles as well as the more modern kiltpins, bracelets, pendants, earrings and cuff links using traditional decorative elements.

1. Frank Adam, *Clans, Septs and Regiments of the Scottish Highlands*, Johnston and Bacon, Edinburgh, 1970, p. 332.
2. *Ibid.*, p. 363.
3. I. F. Grant, *Highland Folk Ways*, Routledge, and Kegan Paul, London, 1961, p. 335.
4. *Ibid.*, p. 322.
5. Donald Wintersgill, *Scottish Antiques*, Johnston and Bacon, Edinburgh, 1977, p. 33.
6. *Ibid.*, p. 36.

Two traditional designs – the plaid pin (left) and the luckenbooth brooch (right).

5. Making Music

Harps

In August 1564 Mary, Queen of Scots, was the guest of the Earl of Atholl. Great efforts were made to please and entertain the young queen: 2000 head of deer were driven through the glen before her, and a competition for harpers was staged. The prize was a small and beautifully finished harp. This instrument, now known as the 'Queen Mary Harp', survives and may be seen in the National Museums of Scotland in Queen Street, Edinburgh. This and another instrument called the Lamont Harp, which dates from around 1464, are the oldest known surviving Scottish harps – although the harp, or clarsach, is in fact one of the oldest of the musical instruments known to Scotland.

While the clarsach almost certainly originated in Ireland, the Welsh and Scots learnt the skills of the clarsach and took them as their own. At the Celtic court, the clarsach-playing bard was a valued figure, and by the twelfth century a Welsh monk and scholar, Giraldus Cambrensis, wrote, 'In the opinion of many, Scotland has not only equalled Ireland her teacher in music, but has prevailed over and surpassed her, so that they look to that country [Scotland] as the fountain of this art.'[1]

The difference between a harp and a clarsach is debatable. Some historians believe the two terms were completely interchangeable, though one account written anonymously in 1597 asserts of the Scots that

> They delight in musicke, but chiefly in Harpes, and *Clairschoes* after their fashion. The strings of their Clairschoes are made of brasse wyar, and the strings of the Harpes of sinews, which strings they strike either with their nayles growing long, or else with an instrument appointed for that use.[2]

(Cutting the nails of a harper was a common punishment for misdemeanours.) Others maintain that the wire-strung instrument was the Highland clarsach, the gut-strung instrument the Lowland harp. In the sixteenth century, harps were highly decorated. The historian, George Buchanan, wrote in 1582, '... their grand ambition is to adorn their harps with great quantities of silver and gems, those who are too poor to afford jewels substituting crystal in their stead.'[3]

Despite the popularity of the instrument, little survives in the way of written harp music, though many tunes originally composed for the harp were probably taken over by the fiddle and the pipes. Many songs, too, would originally have been adapted to the harp by which they were undoubtedly accompanied. Although the harp was the dominant instrument in Scotland for centuries, harpers, unlike pipers and fiddlers, have left few records of the great exponents of the instrument. Some apocryphal tales linger on. The story is told of a mountain road (now Harper's Pass) on the Island of Mull where a harper, freezing with his wife on a cold winter's journey, broke up his harp and burnt it to provide warmth. The wife later proved faithless, and the irate harper cursed, 'Fool that I was to burn my harp for her' – now a local saying to the ungrateful. One

Above: A revolutionary new semitone mechanism has been designed by Mark Norris of Peebles for use on the clarsach.

(Michael Siebert)

Opposite: Alastair Hardie (left) and Angus Grant, two of Scotland's best known fiddle players.

(Della Matheson)

of the few harpers we know anything factual about is Rory Dall – Blind Rory – who was born Roderick Morison on the Island of Lewis around 1660. The victim of smallpox as a young student, Rory lost his sight and turned, as was common among the blind, to music. Devoting himself to a study of the instrument, he travelled to Ireland; on his return, he was appointed harper to the Chief of Macleod, where he stayed for many years. The tradition of maintaining a harper as part of the household in baronial establishments lingered on into the eighteenth century.

For almost 150 years the harp was out of favour. Around 1891 Lord Archibald Campbell, an enthusiast about Gaelic culture, ordered a bagpipe-maker in Edinburgh to make three small clarsachs for him, and later had six made by a Glasgow piano-maker. Other clarsachs made at this time were modelled on an old description and were ornate, incorporating carving and decoration, semi-precious stones and rock crystal. One such harp is on display at the Highland Folk Museum at Kingussie. Lord Campbell, the first President of *An Comunn Gaidhealach*, the organisation devoted to the support and promotion of Gaelic language and culture, proposed a clarsach competition at the first Gaelic Mod in 1892. But it was a lady, Patuffa Kennedy Fraser, whose enthusiasm for the small harp inspired the contemporary renaissance of interest in the instrument. From 1914 she became well known for her singing and playing – to the troops in World War I, then on concert tours in the States and in Europe.

At that time, there appear to have been no clarsach-makers in Scotland. Patuffa Kennedy Fraser bought her instrument from a London maker, George Morley – whose entire stock, clearly destined for the Irish market, was painted green and decorated with shamrocks. John Egan of Dublin, made Irish harps of a different design, much sought after for their tone. Henry Briggs, a Yorkshire violin-maker who lived in Scotland, began to take an interest in the clarsach, and made many fine instruments.

The greatest problem with harps is their enormous string tension. Most stringed instruments have some downward pressure on the sound-board, so that it is possible to make the sound-board itself quite thin, allowing maximum resonance. With the harp, all the strings pull directly on the sound-board.

One of the most inventive of contemporary makers is Mark Norris of Peebles who feels that 'because so much of the harp of the past has been lost to us, there is no 'standard' with which to conform. Harp-makers, unlike violin-makers with the great Italians as their models, can be free to experiment.'

Norris's efforts have been directed to combating the effect of the tension while still allowing the sound-board to resonate. In contrast to the wire-strung Renaissance and Medieval harps made, for example, by Tim Hobrough near Inverness, where the sound-box is hollowed out of a single piece of wood, Norris's sound-box may comprise many different pieces. His greatest innovation is the 'lute-backed' harp, where the sound-box is made from twelve separate staves of around $\frac{1}{8}$in (3mm) in thickness, sandwiched by contrasting decorative inlays. The staves are attached to a skeleton which has been preformed in a specially designed mould. 'The staved back is stronger than you would imagine, because the joins are being pulled *together* by the tension of the strings. The staving process is difficult and time consuming, but this way it is possible to get a very thin, and therefore very resonant, sound-box.'

Holes are then cut in the back for stringing, and to allow the sound to escape, and the sound-board – always spruce – is added. The sound-board is tapered from around $\frac{1}{4}$in (5mm) at the bottom to $\frac{1}{16}$in (1·5mm) at the top, and is glued and screwed on to the side rails of the skeleton. A strip down the centre of both back and front reinforces it at the point of stringing.

The main frame of the harp 'may look elaborate, but is in fact very much simpler.' It is shaped using a template and cut with a band-saw. The major part to be shaped is the shoulder where it joins the sound-box, which must be widened by means of lamination. There is only one join, which takes a huge amount of stress and must be very strong. Norris uses a mortice-and-tenon join, reinforced inside and invisibly by a metal plate. The frame is then decorated with a thin inlay near the outer edge, to add an illusion of delicacy, and fitted to the sound-box offset by two and a half degrees to accommodate perpendicular stringing. At no point is it glued – at the shoulder two locating pins position it, at the foot, a single bolt. It is held in place first and foremost by the tension of the strings.

The rest of the work – 'much more than you would think' – goes into the metal parts for holding and tuning the strings (33 strings in Norris's harps) and in the finish. 'Of the five weeks I take to make the harp, I will probably spend a full week just putting on the finish.

This will involve at least five coats of cellulose lacquer, rubbed down and sanded ever more finely until the finish is perfect.' The most recent development has been the invention of a semi-tone mechanism which allows the alteration of each string by one half tone by the simple flick of a lever – a mechanism which is easy to use and bypasses the problems inherent in the old system.

Modern small harps such as those made by Mark Norris are increasingly in demand, though not as many are played by full-time professional musicians as he would like. The revival of interest in the harp, however, is still in its infancy. Norris's wife, Savourna Stevenson, is a noted exponent of the small harp; her group 'Harp Nouveau' has taken the clarsach into new realms. Norris's own work on the development of an electric harp may well take the ancient clarsach well into the fields of contemporary rock or jazz music as an instrument of great range and versatility. It would be a fitting tribute to the staying power of this most ancient of instruments.

Fiddles

There are four qualifications necessary to greatness in violin-making. First, some training in the use of fine edge tools; second, the artistic faculty – that is, the power to conceive and draw, or paint, or work out graceful designs; third, the ability to test and select wood of the best acoustic properties, and reject all that is not musical toned; and fourth, the power to play the violin, and so be able to test and adjust the instrument before it has been completely finished.

John Henderson, a fiddle maker from Broxburn, c. 1890.
(National Museums of Scotland)

So wrote William Honeyman in 1910 in his introduction to his treatise on Scottish violin-makers.[4]

It is unusual, though, at least among contemporary makers, to find the ability both to play and to make. One exception is Donald Riddell of Clunes near Inverness.

You can only make a violin mathematically to a certain point, then you must use your ear. Tap the back of the fiddle and the front. They are tuned together in a certain relationship; then you get the *tone*. If it's not quite right, you must take off a tiny part.

Riddell served his time – like the famous Matthew Hardie of the eighteenth century – as a cabinetmaker, and was self taught as a player. 'I made my first fiddle before I went to school, though heaven knows what it was like. Now it's my greatest pleasure. The prices I charge are in no way realistic, but I do it because I have to. It's in me.'

The back, sides and necks of Donald Riddell's fiddles are made from sycamore. When he can get the wood, he uses 12,000-year-old bog fir for the fronts, preserved in the acidic peat bogs which arrest the normal processes of decay. Such an instrument, claims Riddell, 'has tonal properties quite distinct from any other. It's a tincture that is absent from the tone of a normal fiddle.'

The greatest of all Scottish fiddle-makers, Matthew Hardie, the so-called 'Scottish Stradivari' (born Edinburgh 1755) was another who used old wood when he could find it. According to one tale,

Hardie was one day, in the year 1821, walking past a field on the Cramond Road when he noticed a weather-beaten paling slab lying on the ground, and, picking it up and noticing its lightness, he balanced it on one finger and struck it with a stone to test the tone. 'What a splendid fiddle breast this will make,' he remarked to his companion. Carrying the slab under his arm he presently stopped at a farm house for a glass of milk, and, being invited into the kitchen to drink it, soon noticed a very old baking board of maple propped on the dresser, which he examined with the most eager interest. 'I see, mistress, ye have a fine fiddle here,' he remarked to the woman of the house. 'A fiddle!' she replied in astonishment. 'There never was sic a thing in the house.' 'Oh yes, there is, but it's well hidden; yet I want to buy it,' answered Hardie. 'If ye can find a fiddle in this house you're welcome to it for

nothing,' answered the woman, when Hardie at once seized upon the old baking-board and said – 'Thank ye, mem; it's inside this baking board and wearying to get out, so I'll e'en take ye at your word. The breast o' her is here,' and he showed her the old paling slab. Next day he sent a bran (sic) new baking-board to the good wife, which highly delighted her, and in due time the hidden fiddle was cut from its covering, and proved to be one of his finest instruments.[5]

Violins built by the great violin-makers of the past have all been rebuilt – the necks have been reangled, fingerboards lengthened to give a bigger range, strengthening added inside to take the increased strain, the base bar strengthened and so on – but contemporary violins follow the same basic pattern as the violins developed by Amati and his followers in Italy from the mid-sixteenth to the late seventeenth centuries. Stringed instruments were common in Scotland certainly from the twelfth century; some were imported, it is thought, by Crusaders returning from the East. Early fiddles may have been flat, without the characteristic arched body of later designs. Stone carvings in Melrose Abbey, which was started around 1136, and at Dunfermline Abbey (1400–1500) show fiddle type instruments, both played by female figures.

Mary, Queen of Scots, recorded the French historian Brantome in 1560, had occasion to hear the fiddle played by a band of loyal citizens:

'There came under her window five or six hundred citizens of the town who gave her a concert of the vilest fiddles and *little rebecs*, which are as bad as they can be in that country. Ah! What a melody it was! What a lullaby for the night!'[6]

The Queen, it is said, thanked the band, but retired to a quieter part of the house. Samuel Pepys was another listener to Scottish fiddle music who did not greatly appreciate its qualities. Visiting Lord Lauderdale, then Secretary of State for Scotland, in 1666, he records,

'At supper, one of his servants played upon the Viallin some Scotch tunes only, several of them the best of their country, as they seemed to esteem them, by their praising and admiring of them. But, Lord! the strangest ayres that ever I heard in my life, and all of one cast.'[7]

The violins which Pepys heard would in all probability have been based on the Italian

Cremona instruments, for it was after the Restoration of 1660 that Amati violins began to find their way to Scotland. Scottish fiddlers were 'quick to see its possibilities as an instrument for their native folk music in its flexibility and incisive tone quality.'[8] Written fiddle music began to come into existence, as it was the custom of fiddlers to record their own repertoire in manuscript books. Such books included popular contemporary airs and songs, as well as dance music. The Strathspey

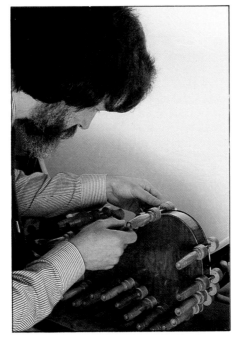

Gordon Stevenson is an Edinburgh-based violin maker. Here he is seen finishing the repair studs on the front of a violin which has been cracked (top left), fitting a hand made maple bridge to an old violin (bottom left), gluing the front onto a violin using closing clamps (top right), and fitting traditionally stained boxwood pegs (bottom right).
(Ian Southern/*Craftwork* magazine)

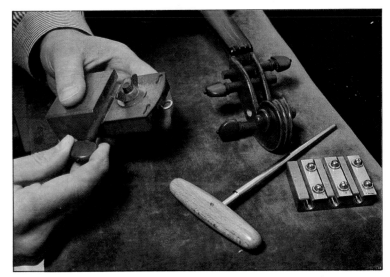

music with which the fiddle has become so closely associated in Scotland did not begin to make its appearance in printed form until the latter part of the eighteenth century.

Perhaps the most famous of all fiddlers was Niel Gow, son of a plaid weaver, born at Inver in Perthshire in 1727. Gow's talent as a fiddler was clearly exceptional, and the demand for his services was enormous. Gow left behind him a substantial repertoire of compositions, many dance tunes – strathspeys, reels and jigs – and exhibition pieces.

Culturally, Shetland's musical heritage was very different from that of Scotland, but the popularity of fiddle music there goes back a very long way. A writer in 1809 noted that 'among the peasantry almost *one in ten* can play the violin.'[9] The antecedent of the violin was an instrument called a gue, similar in appearance to the violin but with two strings only, and of horsehair. Links with Norway were always strong – and still are – and many characteristic Shetland tunes are Norwegian in derivation. Cultural interchange was promoted also by the whaling ships from Greenland, which traditionally carried a fiddler on board; such fiddlers would meet and exchange their tunes, many of which subsequently found their way into the standard Shetland repertoire. There was certainly an association with Ireland, too, and the noted contemporary fiddler and composer, Tom Anderson, recounted that he was able to join with Irish fiddlers in tunes which he knew as Shetland.[10]

The cost of the materials is a substantial part of the cost of a contemporary violin. The figuring of the wood is important, and can be difficult to find. It is not always possible to know just how the wood will look at the time that the tree is bought. The pine for the front is often imported from Germany or Switzerland, and ebony is costly. The time involved adds considerably to the cost of the instrument – with around 70 different parts to be made and assembled, 150 to 200 hours' work go into the making.

The ribs are bent with a hot iron, then held in place in a specially constructed mould, glued together with anchor blocks and strengthened with strips of wood called linings. The back and breast of the violin are shaped by means of planes, gouges and scrapers to the characteristic arched form. The perfect finish is achieved by means of scrapers, not sandpaper, which tears the fibres of the wood and clogs its pores. The purfling (an inlaid decoration) which follows the contour of the violin also acts to further strengthen the structure. It consists of a fine strip of white wood sandwiched between two layers of black fibre. It is inserted into a narrow groove and glued in place before the back is glued to the ribs. The front has, in addition, the decorative f-holes, which allow the free vibration of the instrument and the escape of the sound, and the bass bar which runs the length of the front, strengthening it at the point where there is greatest pressure – under the strings. Once the body of the violin is completed, work on the neck and the scroll can start, using carving tools and templates. When the neck is securely glued to the body, the critical process of varnishing can begin.

The varnish is crucial to the final tonal quality of the fiddle, as well as contributing substantially to its appearance. In 1886 a Scotsman, James Whitelaw, who was not a fiddle-maker but was in the drug trade, developed an amber based varnish which was a marked improvement on the spirit varnishes then available.

> When the wood is sloped to an angle of 30 or 35 degrees from the spectator it shows on every light veining of the wood a peculiarly beautiful golden sheen or bronzed reflection. It is also transparent as some of the ancient deep-hued stained glass; it seems, indeed, to lie like a skin of that glass upon the surface of the wood.[11]

Alas, the secret of Whitelaw's varnish died with him. Today's varnishes are usually linseed-oil based, and are slow to dry. Lacking the sunshine of Italy, modern science has come to the aid of makers in colder parts of the world with a cabinet with fluorescent tubes which dries each coat in 24 hours instead of, sometimes, two or three weeks. Ten or twelve coats will be applied.

Fitting up the violin brings the making to an end; the sound-post, which carries the sound through from the front to the back, is added in a delicate operation; it is threaded through the f-holes and held in place purely by tension. The pegs, fingerboard, tailpiece, bridge and chin rest are then added, completing the process.

The sound of an instrument improves the more it is played, and the older it is. Says Donald Riddell, 'It takes at least 150 hours to make a fiddle – and 50 years to play it in.'

Bagpipes

From the first century AD to the fifteenth, the declamations of the bard accompanied by the clarsach served as 'incitement to battle'. But long before harps left the battlefield, the Great Highland bagpipe, the *piob mhor* which may be heard seven miles away, had effectively taken over as an inspiration for bravery. One bard, understandably bitter about his loss of status, composed (in Gaelic) a satire on the pipes: 'An overblown pig's bladder, grunt, grunt, grunt! . . . like a diseased heron, full of spittle, long limbed and noisy, with an infected chest like that of a grey curlew.'[12]

Bagpipes have featured in the music of many countries over the centuries, and were by no means exclusively a Scottish instrument. It is possible that the bagpipe arrived in Scotland from ancient Egypt; or they may have been

developed from pipes used by Roman soldiers – or quite possibly the instrument was evolved independently in this remote land. Early pipes were certainly quite different from the pipes of today. They would have had only one drone, and the bag was probably a pig's bladder; later, a second drone was added, the third drone by the end of the seventeenth century. At this point in history, bagpipes were played over most of Europe, and certainly pipers were commonplace in England both in the country-side and the court – there are references to the payment of pipers in English court accounts of Edward III, in 1334, and Henry VIII, himself a fine composer and musician, left five sets of bagpipes at his death in 1547. Quite possibly there were English pipers at the Scottish court, too, though it seems that worsening relations between the two countries by 1507 had led to the paying off of all 'Inglis' pipers, leaving only Scots, Italians and French.

Conscientiously, James IV paid off all his debts to his pipers before he marched for Flodden in 1513; tradition has it that the town piper of Jedburgh, Hastie, played his bagpipes on the battlefield. He managed to escape death, and his pipes were handed down by successive generations to the late eighteenth century after which they disappeared.

The pipes were not merely instruments for war, however. The rising popularity of the bagpipes was reflected in Scotland by the emergence in the sixteenth century of the 'town pipers'. These pipers were public ser-vants, maintained by a levy on the rich. They wore the town livery, often had their own free house, and their duties included waking the town daily – usually around four am – and playing out the day around six or seven in the evening. In the Lowlands, where the custom was most strongly upheld, the piper's duties included playing at the annual Riding of the Marches ceremonies, at horse races and fairs, at weddings and at funerals, and possibly also at the harvest.

Increasingly, though, the pipes became the instrument of the Highlands, and it was there that the *piobaireachd* ('pibroch' means pipe music) which is the classical music of the pipes, was evolved. This complex form of music added to the pipe repertoire of dance tunes and short airs, and gave it an authority and dignity which laid the foundation for the remarkable strength and popularity of the instrument through to the present day.

There are many noted names in the history

'Highland Dance' shows Niel Gow (seated), possibly the most famous of all Scottish fiddle players.

(National Galleries of Scotland)

of pipe music; the best known is perhaps MacCrimmon. The MacCrimmons of Skye were hereditary pipers to the Clan MacLeod. Noted for their skill in performance, the MacCrimmons also developed a reputation for teaching, and pupils who attended their College on Skye (there were other such colleges) received tuition for at least seven years and for anything up to twelve years.

The most serious threat to the continued existence of the pipes was the prohibition of the instrument after the Jacobite Rising of 1745. Adding their powerful and emotive exhortation to the fearsome and renowned Highland 'charge' which won the Jacobite army so many successes, the pipes were classified as 'an instrument of war' after the resounding defeat of Prince Charles's ragged army at Culloden, and as such were proscribed. In addition, few of the great clan chiefs who had maintained a hereditary piper before the Jacobite Risings could afford to do so after 1745. Many had fled to France, and those who remained had their powers over their clansmen much diminished. Two major factors saved the pipes from extinction. First, the Highland Society of London, a group of exiled

Scotsmen who had a keen interest in preserving Highland culture, introduced piping competitions.

Second, and perhaps the force which had an even greater influence on the development of the instrument, was the raising of new Highland Regiments. Playing on the fierce inbred pride and loyalty of the Scots, the government in London allowed these regiments to have their own pipers and drummers. The pipe bands of the army both ensured the continuance of the pipes as an instrument with a strong Scottish identity and began the process of formalising and restricting the instrument into the rigid rules of acceptable play which exist today.

The process of formalising the music of the pipes affected also the making of the instrument. Entries in pipemaker's catalogues showed the availability of up to seventeen different kinds and sizes of pipe, and included the bellows-blown 'Lowland' pipes as well as the dominant Great Highland pipes. The Lowland pipes had virtually disappeared by the end of the nineteenth century, but today there is a revival of interest in the instrument, and the beginnings of innovation in pipe

Opposite: a finished set of pipes made by William Sinclair and Son, Leith.

(Michael Siebert)

Below: racks of hand turned drone pieces stand awaiting assembly.

(Michael Siebert)

music. The 'caul pipes' or cold pipes – that is, bellows-blown – have become so popular in recent years that several craftsmen have begun to make them, and a Lowland and Border Piping Society was formed in 1983.

Little information exists about the making of early pipes. Almost certainly they would have been fashioned from local materials, from laburnum or box, the bags from sheepskin, the mounts from horn. Even locally-fashioned instruments would have been expensive, and there is plenty of evidence of broken chanters, bound, whipped and mended in ingenious ways. Nowadays a cracked chanter would be discarded as useless. There would always have been roaring trade in

second-hand instruments, and pipes by makers such as MacDougalls, who worked in Aberfeldy in Perthshire from 1792 to 1857, have always been much sought after.

Today's bagpipes bear little resemblance to their grunting pig-bladder antecedents. Techniques, handed down through generations, have given way to modern technology, and the contemporary bagpipe is a sophisticated, precision-made instrument, with more than 40 separate components. Almost nothing of the instrument is local: the wood and the ivory come from Africa; the cowhide is from Argentina; the sheepskins are from Norway; the plastic is Italian; and the cane for the reeds is Spanish.

The skill in making a good set of bagpipes lies in the care in the wood-turning processes.
(Michael Siebert)

One well-known Edinburgh maker is Alastair Sinclair, whose father and grandfather started their Leith-based business in 1933:

The best wood for the drones and the chanter is African blackwood, but it's extremely hard to come by these days. It comes ready cut now – if you can get it at all. We used to cut it ourselves on a band-saw. It was so hard that a new blade would last no more than twenty minutes. The best wood comes from Tanzania. We can use other woods – Canadian maple is good – but the public don't like it because it isn't the traditional dark colour.

Each set of pipes has fourteen pieces of wood to be turned – five stocks into which the drones are set, the chanter, the blowstick, the three parts of the bass drone and two tenor drones each with two parts.

The drones are turned on a lathe to a rough finish, then holes are put through using big hand drills. We have to make a lot of our own tools because nothing is in standard sizes. The size of the hole is important, of course, but in my opinion it's the *relationship* of all the sizes in the drone which gives the sound, and the finish. If you can get a rifle-barrel finish, you'll get a good sound.

The chanter itself is the most exacting piece to make, and the finished chanter has very thin walls and great precision is required to bore it out. It is the chanter which will largely determine the final timbre of the instrument, and heavy fingering will also take its toll of the finish. It is for that reason that Sinclair's wax-finish the chanter, while the turned wood of the drones and the stocks is finished with a coat of polyurethane varnish which dries well on the blackwood. Modern chanters differ from chanters of 60 or 80 years ago in having a higher pitch, and being thinner and better finished.

The ferrules or outer mounts which fit on to the drones or stocks are now most commonly made of an imitation ivory, but elephant ivory is still used, too. They can also be made from silver, engraved or plain. They are intended as decoration, but serve also to prevent the end of the wood from splitting.

When all the turned pieces are completed, they are 'mounted'. Some joints are threaded, to make them airtight, others, such as where the drones, chanter and blowstick fit into their stocks, are hemped. Threading is also done on the drone slides where they need to be moveable for tuning.

The reeds, which are fitted into the three drones and the chanter, are made from cane. The lengths of cane are divided into four strips, split along their length and mitred at one end. After they are guillotined to an elongated triangle, they are chiselled by hand to a thickness of $\frac{1}{24}$in (1mm). The cane is then soaked, hand bound with thermal waxed thread and held together by a copper staple, then sanded and varnished with shellac to keep it airtight. Most pipe-makers will obtain their supplies of reeds from specialist reed-makers.

The final component is the bag itself. Pipe bags intended for use in Scotland or other cold countries are made fron sheepskin. Sheepskin absorbs moisture and keeps the pipes and reeds drier. In hotter countries the pipes benefit from a bag made of cowhide, which sheds water which is blown through the instrument, and therefore helps to stop the reeds drying out. The bags are all hand-sewn with thick waxed thread, then the stocks are tied tightly on with waxed hemp.

A piper buying a set of pipes will be looking for a free and steady vibration of sound, and a compatibility between the drones and the reeds. The finish may be important aesthetically, but in the end, it is how the pipes sound which determines their quality.

1. Giraldus Cambrensis, 'Topographica Hibernia' quoted in Henry George Farmer, *Music in Medieval Scotland*, London.
2. Francis Collinson, *The National and Traditional Music of Scotland*, Routledge and Kegan Paul, London 1966, p. 230.
3. George Buchanan, *History* 1582, quoted in Frank Adam, *Clans, Septs and Regiments of the Scottish Highlands*, Johnston and Bacon, Edinburgh and London, 1908 (1975 edition) p. 417.
4. William C. Honeyman, *Scottish Violin Makers, Past and Present*, Dundee 1890, p. 15.
5. *Ibid.*, p. 54.
6. Collinson, *op. cit.*, p. 201.
7. *The Diaries of Samuel Pepys*, 28 July 1666.
8. Collinson, *op. cit.*, p. 203.
9. A. E. Edmonstone, quoted in Collinson, *op. cit.*, p. 253.
10. *Ibid.* p. 259.
11. *Ibid.*, p. 99.
12. Francis Collinson, *The Bagpipe*, Routledge and Kegan Paul, London 1975, p. 186.

6. The Sporting Scot

To Curle on the Ice, does greatly please,
Being a Manly *Scotish* Exercise,
It Clears the Brains, stirs up the Native Heat,
And gives a gallant Appetite for Meat.[1]

Curling

Scotland has a number of traditional sports and more than one can be traced back several centuries. Curling, often likened to 'bowls on ice', is one of these. Mention of it first appears in records from Paisley Abbey near Glasgow with the example of a monk who, in 1541, challenged the Abbot's deputy to a tournament on ice. One of the earliest descriptions of the game, however, was by Thomas Pennant in his *Tour of Scotland* in 1772:

> . . . it is an amusement of the winter and played on ice, by sliding from one mark to another, great stones of forty to seventy pounds in weight, of a hemispherical form, with an iron or wooden handle at top. The object of the player is to lay his stone as near to the mark as possible, to guard that of his partner, which had been well laid before, or to strike off that of his antagonist.[2]

The earliest curlers used stones collected from stream beds or hillsides, the only crafting involved being the chipping of finger holes. In the seventeenth century bent iron handles were added and many stones, because of their irregular shape, assumed identifying names like 'the Egg' or 'the Baron'. Some of these stones, compared with present-day standards, required exceptional strength, weighing in excess of 100lb (45·36kg).

In 1838 the game was formalised by the Grand Caledonian Curling Club – the word 'Royal' was added in 1843 when Prince Albert became patron. This Club laid down the rules of curling. The game is played with pairs of stones and by two sides of four players each. Players aim the stones towards a circular target drawn on the ice, brushing the path of the stone as it travels. Nowadays, the stones themselves must not weigh more than 44lb (19·96kg) or exceed a circumference of 36in (91·4cm). And the game, which was traditionally played on frozen lochs has moved indoors to curling-rinks. The one exception to this remains the 'bonspiel', a grand match played out-of-doors whenever the weather becomes

Opposite: fly rods crafted by David Norwich develop in a number of stages beginning with the splitting of bamboo culms.

(Michael Siebert)

Left and below: some of Scotland's early curling enthusiasts had to be men of great strength for the irregular-shaped stones could weigh as much as 100lbs.

In the days when marble was still quarried from Ailsa Craig, the roughly shaped stones were piled on the beach, prior to being transported across the water.

(Andrew Kay and Co.)

cold enough to produce at least 6in (15·2cm) of ice. The world championships in curling are scheduled annually at different venues.

At one time there were twelve different makers of curling-stones in Scotland. Today only one Scottish company crafts these granite stones, and 40 per cent of their output is exported to one of the world's newest converts to the game, Japan. Andrew Kay and Company of Mauchline, Ayrshire also export to ice-rinks in Canada, Switzerland, France and Germany. Kay's and a Welsh manufacturer are believed to be the only suppliers of curling-stones in the world.

The Mauchline firm first began crafting curling-stones in 1864 when a young stone-mason, Andrew Kay, became captivated by the ancient sport. Curlers, then using unpolished hunks of granite with crude handles, were demanding more polished stones and Kay devised a manufacturing process using a few hand tools. His first pair of Kay's Excelsior curling-stones were made in a small shop at The Haugh, just one mile from the present factory in Mauchline and his business prospered almost immediately. Regrettably

Kay died young, at the age of 32, and probably from the physical demands of the job, but his widow continued the business with the help of a young lawyer, James Wyllie. Wyllie eventually bought out the business in 1926, and today his grandson and namesake carries on the tradition.

Some of the best granite for curling-stones was originally obtained from Ailsa Craig, a well-known island off the Ayrshire coast. Quarrying on the island, however, was difficult. Men had to be landed there, blast the stone and then hand-cut it, before it could be transported across to the mainland in a small boat – a very expensive procedure. In the mid-sixties, efforts were made to discover new supplies of suitable granite, and after much testing and research Kay's decided to use granite quarried from the Trevor Mountain in Wales. This is still the main source of supply.

When lumps of granite arrive at Kay's from the Welsh quarry, the first step in their crafting is the rough cut. A finished stone which weighs 40lb (18·14kg) plus (but not more than 44 (19·96kg) begins as a block of 100lb (45·36kg) in weight. After the rough cut, a hole is bored in the centre with an electric drill and the stone is then turned on a power-lathe. At the conclusion of this stage the stone is approaching its required weight. Next it is ground, then polished by hand with a variety of abrasives and water. The distinctive shiny surface of a curling-stone is broken only by the striking band around the middle, which is left rough and unpolished. It is this band which takes the impact of hits by other stones and it receives special attention in the crafting: the striking band is given its finishing touches with a hand-hammer. A fine line is then engraved at one side of the band to help remind the curler that the stone should be turned periodically to spread wear and tear.

Power-driven lathes and drills have considerably eased the crafting of curling-stones since Andrew Kay set up his original shop next to a river so that he could harness water-power to drive his machinery. No step in the process, however, is automated. The lathes required for turning the hard granite now come from an engineering firm in Kilmarnock in Ayrshire, but Kay's still fire their own forge at least three times a week in order to hone the cutting edges. A total of ten hours is required to craft each stone, and each of the five stages of crafting requires a one-year training period to master. Kay's currently employ a workforce of twelve and most of the men have been trained in at least two, if not three of the five crafting processes.

The durability of the stones – and Kay's guarantee theirs for 50 years – is one reason why so few makers of curling-stones remain. And curling itself is a game which has fluctuated in popularity. Eight years ago Kay's responded to a Canadian initiative to attract young people to the game, by making junior stones which weigh only 25lb (11·34kg). These are light enough to be handled by six and seven-year-olds. The firm has changed and improved its product in other ways. The handles of the stones have altered through the years – from iron to brass, to chrome, to plastic. Kay's now offer a range of eight different coloured handles with matching

Polishing the granite stone with water and abrasives.

Finished stones in the Andrew Kay and Company factory in Mauchline.

brushes to make sighting easier for the team members. And the firm have recently added a new square key-locking feature which helps overcome the problem of the handle slackening during play. Kay's also recondition old stones.

Golf

Golf is said to have been invented by the Dutch. The Scots may find this hard to accept but it was unquestionably the Scots who developed the game and exported it to a grateful world. The earliest written mention of golf in Scotland is in 1457 (the Dutch were playing it in the thirteenth century), and the original 13 rules by which the game was governed were formalised in Edinburgh in 1744. Golf never really developed, however,

until 1848 when the rubber golf ball was invented. Prior to that time, the game was played with the 'feathery' – a leather ball stuffed with wet feathers, which had an unfortunate tendency to shatter when struck with an iron. These balls were costly to make not only in terms of money but for reasons of health: the makers who packed the feathers tightly into the casing did so with the aid of an iron brace fixed to the chest. As for the price, at four shillings (20p) a ball cost as much as a club.

The discovery of gutta-percha in Malaysia in 1843 had a dramatic impact on the game. Gutta-percha balls could be made simply by immersing the hard material in hot water for softening, then rolling it by hand. It hardened as it dried into a dark yellow/brown ball and though at first it did not fly properly, this was soon remedied by indenting the ball with a hammer. Later, in the 1880s, the 'gutty' or hard, composite ball appeared – so hard that it could shatter the head of a wooden club. In 1898 when the Haskell core-wound rubber ball was invented in America the feathery and gutty passed into history. Nostalgic lovers of golfing memorabilia, however, will be glad to know that the feathery is still being made as a collector's item. William MacKay, a leather craftsman in Invergordon near Inverness, makes featheries for Golf Classics of St Andrews, a firm which has been making traditional hickory-shafted putters since 1970. The featheries are made by Mr MacKay in the old way – but without the chest brace. He uses cowhide for the balls, packing each with the traditional measure of wet feathers – a lum-hat (top hat) full.

The making of golf-clubs is, of course, as old as the game itself. And in St Andrews, the universally accepted 'home of golf', club-making is a familiar business. Auchterlonies is a firm that has been making clubs since 1895. Golfing historians will also associate the name with some champion players – the Open Championship at Prestwick in Ayrshire in 1893 was won by Willie Auchterlonie and his brother, Laurie, won the American Open in 1902. These brothers, two of the six sons born to a master plumber in St Andrews, first played golf with bent sticks and corks: 'We played from one side of the street to the other, backwards and forwards alternately, making the gas lamp posts there do duty for holes and the way we counted was to try to touch each post in the least number of strokes.'[3]

Even when the brothers graduated to more

Reproducing a classic putter, from start to finish.

(Michael Siebert)

sophisticated clubs, these were often makeshift – old heads and assorted shafts joined together by melted gutta-percha and wound with string. Iron clubs were hard to come by, except by barter. A group of two or three youngsters would descend on the local blacksmith and lend a hand turning his manual lathe in return for payment of an old or spoiled iron head. The blacksmith, Bob Wilson, was the first man to make iron club heads in St Andrews – some had the curious feature of a horseshoe nail at the back of the blade. Willie and another brother, Davie, became professional club-makers as did their youngest brother, Tom. Tom's early customers included the Japanese Royal family, who gave him two big orders in the 1920s. One of Tom Auchterlonie's early catalogues, which were printed about 1924, sold irons and putters with a touch of poetic humour:

Whose Putters send the ball most true
And pile up hole on hole for you
By sinking putts right out of view
TOM AUCHTERLONIE!

In 1907 Willie Auchterlonie was already lamenting the introduction of machinery, an advance which he felt was destroying the 'art' of club-making.[4] Instead of hewing out the head of a club from a rough block of wood, this initial task was being undertaken by a lathe, making the only hand-work that of finishing. Most clubs today are made with the help of modern machinery – indeed the clubs themselves, with their steel shafts, are a far remove from those made at the beginning of the century. In recent years, however, several firms have taken a step back in time and have begun making traditional hickory-shafted putters. Auchterlonies is one of these and their workshop in St Andrews, with its plate-glass window to the street, is a public show-case for any who care to watch craftsmen at work.

The hickory-shafted putters crafted today by the firm include: the 'Grand Slam', a copy of a putter made by them in the 1920s, with a laminated maple head, and a reversed calf-skin grip; 'The Classic', made from aged persimmon, a replica of an early nineteenth-century putter; and the 'Presentation' which has a head made from hornbeam.

Aside from the laminated material, almost all the woods used in these traditional putters are imported (the hickory shafts come from

Opposite top: fitting the horn edge to a putter.

Opposite bottom: pouring molten lead into the cavity of the head.

Below: tourists watch the club-making process in Auchterlonies' window.
(Michael Siebert)

South Carolina). The crafting of these putters takes twelve hours, spread over a period of weeks. Lead is used for weighting the putters and horn for protecting the leading edge. The lead is poured hot into the putter head cavity, a step which makes the wood swell. Time is required for the wood to settle down to its normal size and moisture content before other steps in the process can continue. Auchterlonies sub-contract the rough turning of the putter heads and the hickory shafts, but their craftsmen still invest a great deal of time and skill in the some 2600 traditional-style putters that they make each year. Four craftsmen work full time on club-making and two of these are apprentices undertaking a four-year training.

The hickory shafts are finished with a coat of pitch to bring up the grain, then wiped clean and coated with oil and shellac. The heads, which have been filed and sanded from their original rough turning, hollowed and filled with lead and fitted with a horn strip, are then fitted to the shaft. This process can become even more prolonged when the use of power-lathes is omitted. Jim Horsfield, a director of Auchterlonies, who aside from being a golf enthusiast has had experience in wood-turning and carving, makes about four completely handcrafted putters a year. His work is reminiscent of the 'art' which Willie Auchterlonie described in the original crafting – before the use of power machinery. The rough shaping of a block of persimmon, is done with a saw. Coarse filing with a rasp provides

further refinement before the lead infill is undertaken and then the finishing. The investment of time in these putters makes them very much 'special orders' – putters for the golfer who seeks something absolutely original.

Shinty

To the uninformed observer, the game resembles a general mêlée. Indeed, one spectator of the game of shinty, writing in *The Penny Magazine of the Society for the Diffusion of Useful Knowledge* in 1835, had some quite alarming observations to make about this traditional Highland sport which is played with a hard ball and a curved wooden stick, or 'caman':

> Large parties assemble during the Christmas holidays, one parish sometimes making a match against another. In the struggle between the contending players many hard blows are given, and frequently a shin is broken or by a rarer chance some more serious accident may occur. The writer witnessed a match, in which one of the players, having gained possession of the ball, contrived to run a mile with it in his hand, pursued by both his own and the adverse party until he reached the appointed limit, when his victory was admitted. Many of the Highland farmers join with eagerness in the sport, and the laird frequently encourages by his presence this amusement of his labourers and tenants.

The popularity of shinty has waxed and waned over the years. About 30 clubs at present exist in Scotland and most are concentrated in the West and the Highlands. The official shinty organisation is the Camanachd Association, formed in 1893 and its yearly competition for the Camanachd Association

Prize-winning photograph of John MacKenzie of Newtonmore in the 1978 Camanachd Cup shinty final.
(Donald Mackay)

Challenge Cup provides a regular stimulus for the game.

Shinty is played on a field measuring a minimum length of 160yds (146·304m) and a width of 80yds (73·152m). Each team consists of twelve players and a goalkeeper and the game begins with the referee throwing up the ball between two players, who have camans crossed above head level. The purpose of the game is, of course, to put the ball across the opponent's goal-line. Each game lasts 90 minutes with teams playing 45 minutes each way. It is a very physically demanding sport as the handbook of rules of play for the Camanachd Association points out:

. . . it is no pastime for weaklings, or degenerates, nor is it an exercise wherein the slow-witted or dullards will be found to shine. It calls for physical and mental gifts of no mean order. It calls into play practically all the chief muscles of the human body; it requires quickness of eye and sureness of aim; it demands both rapidity and coolness of judgment; and, above all, it calls for perfect control of temper.'

The crafting of camans for shinty is still carried on in Scotland, though in a slightly different manner: the original camans, which were made of a solid wooden shaft and head glued together, have achieved greater durability with the introduction of laminating processes used in the making of skis. As for the complicated process of making shinty-balls – they consist of a cork core, wrapped in wool and then covered with leather – they have become so labour-intensive that their Scottish manufacture has almost completely ceased. With a projected life of only two games, the balls (called the 'leathers') have proved too expensive for the shoemakers and other leather workers who once undertook their production. Nowadays, they come from outwith the country – sometimes from Ireland where hurling (a game similar to shinty but played with slightly different sticks and balls) is an indigenous sport.

The official club-maker to the Camanachd Association is Prolam (Kingussie), a company run by Rudi Prochazka, whose experience in ski manufacture inspired the making of the more durable shinty-sticks now in common use. In the early 1970s, when shinty enthusiasts found their supply of sticks disappearing

Shinty sticks nowadays are made of laminated hickory and finished with linseed oil.

(Rudi Prochazka)

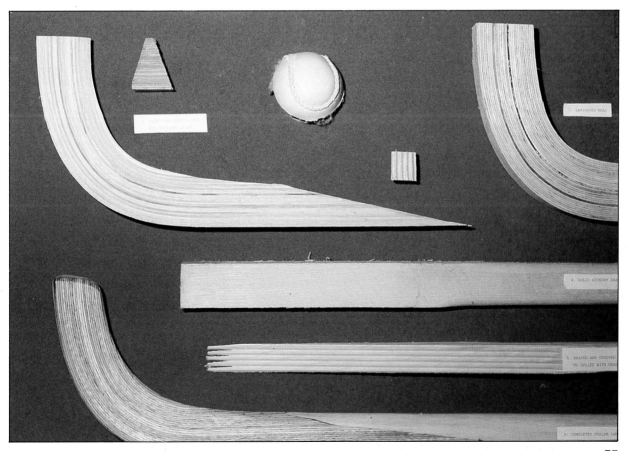

(unlike golf and curling, shinty did not export well and manufacturers declined to make sticks in small quantities), Rudi was asked by Camanchd if he would make some sticks. He had always liked working with wood and his hastily improvised shinty-stick prototype won an immediate order for 200. 'There I was' he now recalls 'with no proper tools, no money and going on holiday. That's what started it all . . .'

Now, in a good year, he will make as many as 1500 shinty-sticks in three different styles, each suitable for a particular team position. He fits in this particular crafting operation during the off-season before winter sports begin, and in between running his sports shop in Kingussie.

An early comment on fly fishing.

(Mr Punch's Scottish Humour, The Educational Book Co. Ltd, no date)

PRETTY DRY

Young Beginner (fishing with dry fly). "Am I keeping my fly properly dry, Duncan?"
Scots Keeper. "Oh, I'm thenkin' she'll be dry enough. She's stickin up in that big willow near by where ye started fishin'."

Hickory wood from America is used for the sticks. The camans must not include metal of any sort and the head of the stick must be of a size that can pass through a 2½in (6·35cm) diameter ring. The first stage in their crafting is cutting – either into shafts or veneers. The shafts of the sticks are shaped by hand-planing and are fitted to the heads by a special interlocking process patented by Rudi. Each head is made of laminated veneers: as many as 32 layers, each ¹⁄₂₄in (1mm) thick, can go into one stick. The veneers are clamped in a press and the resulting laminates cut to size and width. Steam was formerly used to bend the solid heads of shinty-sticks but with the new laminating process, special presses can achieve the required curve. The sticks are finished with a coat of linseed oil and the handles wrapped with canvas tape.

One caman should last at least ten games, says Rudi Prochazka, and so in a normal season of 20 games each player will require at least two. The nature of this robust game thus ensures the future of the specialist craftsman.

Fishing
Fishing rods

'I could get quite lyrical about fly-fishing,' says David Norwich.

I was only nine when I saw a man fly-fishing in the Water of Leith, and I thought it was the most beautiful thing I had ever seen. I went home and cut the middle out of an old seven-foot cane spinning-rod and added a bit of solid fibreglass to the middle to make it bend. I caught trout with it but the action wasn't right. Before that I had been sea-fishing using hand-lines and rods of greenheart, the heavy dense wood that was used before cane became popular.

Scotland's rich endowment of lochs and rivers make fly-fishing a popular sport. And the real enthusiasts know that the graceful arch of the line and the speed with which it is cast depend as much on the taper and flexibility of the rod as on the ability of the angler. 'It requires quite a bit of skill to get it right,' says David Norwich 'but once you have mastered the technique, fly-fishing is marvellous. The casting provides satisfaction in itself – the fishing is an extra bonus.'

David Norwich is a rare craftsman in the fishing fraternity, for he is one of the few who make bamboo fly rods by hand. He does it from an idyllic situation, in a workshop attached to a neat cottage outside Fountainhall, a small village near Galashiels in the Borders. Aside from the view across rolling countryside, there is the added attraction of a stream just a few steps from his garden. His own love of the sport is, of course, what brought him to the craft. Years of experimentation and development have refined his own ideas about the qualities of a good fly rod.

You have to be able to put the line out without any bumps or rolls in the cast and the fly must land like thistle-down. Mass-produced rods usually don't have fine

enough action to do that. In a well-designed rod, the power flows straight down the line through the tip. The rod must be light and responsive, and not feel like a dead weight in the hand – if it does, then the taper is not right.

The all-important taper of the rod calls for precision crafting and the use of a micrometer, which allows Norwich to measure rod sections to within one-thousandth of an inch. This fine measurement is just one step in a process which begins with the selection of quality

Shaping the fly-rod grip.
(Michael Siebert)

bamboo culms from China. Key elements in the selection of good bamboo are colour, appearance, weight and 'feel'. Heating the bamboo bakes out the moisture and strengthens the fibres making the bamboo steely and springy. The heat treatment also creates the rich golden colours.

Once the bamboo culms have been cured, they are split into quarters with a knife and mallet. Six strips are then chosen and roughly shaped in preparation for milling. Special care is taken to mismatch the strips so that no two nodes on the bamboo come together in a finished section – a circumstance which, if allowed, would weaken the rod. The milling process reduces each of the strips to the thinness of a blade of grass, each strip having been cut with a 60-degree triangular angle and checked with a micrometer for accuracy.

Every two-piece bamboo fishing-rod has three sections, a butt and two tips, each of which is assembled and glued with a special resin from the six thin strips. The finishing of

the bamboo sections involves scraping and sanding, and then each section must be further straightened by applying heat. Norwich also makes all of the reel fittings required for the rods, the cork grips and the nickel-silver ferrules. Maria Norwich, David's wife, fits all the rings by hand using fine silk threads. Norwich has evolved his own special techniques for the varnish finish on the rods and each rod is signed with his name.

Norwich's process of building a traditional bamboo fly rod has been further developed with a 'hollow-built' rod, which he describes as the 'ultimate' in fly-rod technology. In order to reduce the weight of the rod and offer an even faster action, Norwich has devised a technique of scalloping each of the six precision tapered strips that make up the rod. It is a process requiring many hours of detailed work, and one which results in the 'Rolls Royce' of rods for the fishing enthusiast. This attention to precision and to perfecting the casting performance of each fly rod makes

Opposite: a selection of traditional salmon flies tied by Pete Blakeley.

Below: David Norwich testing a rod in the stream near his home.

(Michael Siebert)

Norwich reluctant to speculate on the investment of time spent in making a rod: 'It takes as long as it takes,' he says. His rods are exported to America, Japan, Sweden, France and Germany.

Flies

Tying salmon flies has caught the imagination of innumerable anglers, but nowadays the technique seems clouded wth nostalgia. Megan Boyd of Brora in Sutherland, who was awarded a British Empire Medal for teaching children the craft, started tying salmon flies because they used to be 'beautiful things to look at. Today,' she says 'they are not so nice, as one can neither get the feathers nor good materials to work with . . . hair of all sorts has taken the place of feathers for the wings.' One life-long angler who has developed a business out of the nostalgia for old salmon flies is Pete Blakeley of Classic Flies in Langholm, Dumfriesshire. Blakeley is sympathetic to the view first expressed over 70 years ago by T. E. Pryce-Tannatt when he wrote that 'dressing salmon flies . . . is an agreeable way of giving expression to one's sense of the artistic . . .'[5]

Salmon-anglers today use fairly simple hair-wing patterns of flies to attract their fish – flies which in Megan Boyd's estimation rely too much on hair but are perhaps more in keeping with the original intent of replicating a moth. In contrast, the late nineteenth and early twentieth centuries saw a vogue for gaudy salmon-flies with brightly coloured feathers. It is this flamboyant era of salmon-fly design and dressing that Blakeley now replicates for collectors. Since most of the materials he uses are now costly or difficult to obtain, Blakeley does not reproduce the old patterns for actual use. Instead, he mounts them.

A number of colourful and elaborate flies are included among Blakeley's repertoire including such intriguing names as the 'Durham Ranger', 'Thunder and Lightning', the 'Blue Doctor' and the 'Green Highlander'. A connoisseur's collection of famous salmon-fly patterns used on the Rivers Tay, Dee and Spey, feature a 'Black Dog', 'Grey Eagle', 'Lady Caroline' and 'Carron'.

Blakeley first started experimenting with fly-tying about 20 years ago but his interest in the traditional patterns is fairly recent. He can spend an hour or more tying a single fly in his workshop overlooking the River Esk: the biggest challenge to his patience, he says, is marrying the many different feathers. The wings of some classic flies require as many as six different feathers – the 'Jock Scott', an old favourite has some 25 different feathers in its entirety, including dyed swan, barred wood duck and florican bustard. With the exception of dyed swan, Blakeley makes a point of using natural feathers in his work and he follows the traditional method of tying – making the wings of the fly first.

Gunmaking

Scotland's wonderful moorland expanses have always provided sport in the form of grouse and pheasant shooting and deer stalking – a very necessary exercise in terms of game conservation. It is perhaps fitting, therefore, that it was in Scotland that one of the most important innovations in the history of firearms was made.

The percussion gun was invented in 1806 by an Aberdeenshire minister, Alexander Forsyth, and it superseded the old flintlock method of igniting the powder. Forsyth's gun had a tiny hammer which struck a volatile substance and set off an explosion. It was much more reliable than the old flintlock method where a flint struck steel to make a spark, and suffered less from the problem of damp. As a sporting gun it had several advantages, not least its internal ignition mechanism. The old flintlock mechanism involved a small flash and a delay of a few seconds before the gun fired. Such a delay gave the prey time to take evasive action. Forsyth's gun was adopted by the army in 1839.

By the turn of the century, the hammer mechanism had all but disappeared; every gunmaker in Britain was struggling to produce a double-barrelled, side-lock, hammerless ejector-gun. Scottish makers, isolated from mainstream thinking, took their own look at the mechanism, and one Edinburgh firm, John Dickson and Son, came up with a unique design – their round-action gun. First produced in 1887, the round-action gun has proved its worth on the Scottish grouse moors now for 100 years. It is this gun which is made today by Scotland's only surviving gunmaker, David McKay Brown.

The round-action gun has many advantages over the traditional English side-lock guns. Elegant to look at, with no protrusions or squared-off corners, the round-action gun is very streamlined, with the lines flowing from the breech end of the barrels. A single-trigger plate unit houses two complete sets of locks, a safety mechanism, triggers and furniture, where in other guns these are separate units.

*Above: Malcolm Appleby's
engraving of the 'Raven' gun
in progress.*

*Opposite top: David Mackay
Brown at work in his Bothwell
gun shop.*

(Andrea Cringean)

*Opposite bottom: checking the
lock unit.*

(Andrea Cringean)

The action body is a solid construction, which gives great strength and allows for a reduction in size and weight, giving a better balance. It is also very reliable – the bow-type mainsprings are never under full deflection. The ejector mechanisms are powered by coil springs which are very strong, and the top-lever return spring, which operates the bolting-up mechanism, will still function in the field even if a coil breaks.

Hand-made guns of this quality are not cheap (and most serious sportsmen would buy a pair), and 90 per cent of the cost is in the labour. Parts of the gun are machine-tooled, but even the machines have to be designed and made by McKay Brown to his own very specific needs. There are about 80 parts in the gun, and each one is forged and machined in the workshop in Bothwell in Lanarkshire.

Each gun is individually tailored to the needs of the client. The measurements are taken on their local range, using a gun with an adjustable stock to accommodate variations. A tall man will require longer barrels, a broad man requires a 'cast-off' to bring the barrel into line with the master eye. The use to which the gun will be put is important, too; a gun for grouse will have its bores regulated for an effective pattern at 25yds (22·860m), while a gun for high pheasant will have tighter bores for a suitable pattern at perhaps 40yds (36·576m). The weight of the gun is to some

extent a matter of personal preference – a heavier gun will absorb more recoil.

The matter of finish is important, too, and this will be determined before the gunmaking starts. The woodwork – figured walnut – is selected. If a pair is ordered, then the wood must come from the same tree to provide a match of colour and grain structure. The wood itself can cost as much as £1000. Engraving can be selected from a book containing traditional styles, or can be commissioned to suit the client's wishes.

The barrels of the gun are made from Sheffield steel. The tubes are brazed together by the barrel filer, and machined at the breech ends to shoot in at 40yds (36·576m). The ribs are filed separately and tinned to the barrels. The tubes are then provisionally bored.

The steel for the action body also comes from Sheffield, using drop forgings for the major components. The major parts are machined in batches of a dozen at a time. The actioner takes the assembled barrels and joints them into the action body, then bolts up the barrels by fitting the lever, key and bolt. The action body is then roughly shaped – sculpted – in preparation for nitro-proofing. Every gun made in Britain must be tested at a proof-house. There are only two, in Birmingham and in London. McKay Brown's guns are all proofed in London. Proofing involves a visual inspection for defects after which an over-

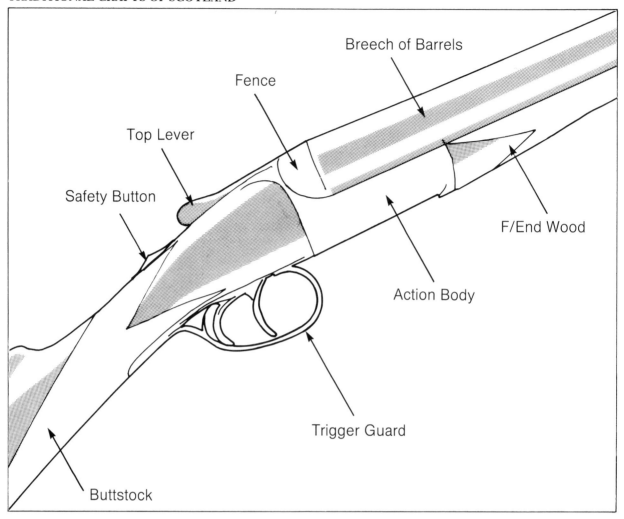

Breech of Barrels

Fence

Top Lever

Safety Button

F/End Wood

Action Body

Trigger Guard

Buttstock

loaded cartridge is fired from each barrel. A further inspection determines if there has been any weakness or movement in the barrel tubes and breech.

The lock unit and the furniture of the gun is assembled into the barrelled action with the correct degree of cast. It is then filed up and prepared for the stocker.

The stocker works in wood alone. The stocks are made from seasoned walnut, at least eight years old. The wood, when bought in (usually from France), is weighed and dated, then weighed again some years later. If it has lost weight, then the wood was green when it was bought. In fact it should gain a little weight, because in Scotland the climate is wetter than in France. When the gun is stocked up, it goes back to the actioner who polishes the metal prior to engraving.

Engraving can take up to three months, depending on the complexity of the work involved. Most of McKay Brown's guns are engraved by Crathes-based engraver, Malcolm Appleby. Appleby is well versed in the traditional patterns, but prefers where possible to develop his art. 'What I am doing is very unusual. These round-action guns are very subtle, and offer wonderful design possibilities. You have to work round them as one design, and they pose quite a design problem. In the end, though, they are much more satisfying.'

Once engraved, the gun is colour hardened. This process gives the mild-steel action body a tough core and a hard case. It must not be brittle, or it will shatter with the first shot. It also produces subtle colour variations which help to inhibit rust. The colours should not be polished off, but allowed to wear off slowly to maintain protection.

After engraving, the gun requires heat treating and finishing. It therefore needs to be case hardened. All the inner working parts need careful heat treatment, with a degree of localised hardening. Certain areas, though, are left almost glass hard for wear and are critical for correct trigger pressure. This kind of work is a true craft, demanding expertise and hand-skill of a kind which modern engineering would find it hard to reproduce.

The guns made in the Bothwell workshop are inimitable by mass-production techniques, and few 'modern' techniques can be adopted in their making. The exceptionally fine quality of their production was acknowledged in 1987 when the Royal Armouries of the Tower of London commissioned 'The Raven Gun' from the McKay Brown/Appleby team. Decorated with the plumage of the ravens which

guard the Tower, the gun is the first commission of the armourer's art for centuries.

1. Alexander Pennecuik, M.D. quoted in John Kerr, *The History of Curling*, David Douglas, Edinburgh 1890, p. 95.
2. Thomas Pennant, *Tour of Scotland*, London 1772, p. 93.
3. Henry Leach (ed.), *Great Golfers in the Making*, Methuen & Co., London, 1907, p. 219.
4. *Ibid.*, p. 220.
5. T. E. Pryce-Tannatt, *How to Dress Salmon Flies*, A. & C. Black, London, 1914, p. 4.

The Punch *view of hunting.*
(Royal Museums of Scotland)

"UNCO CANNY"

Noble Sportsman. "Missed, eh?"
Cautious Keeper. "Weel, a' wadna gang quite sae faur as to say that; but a' doot ye hav'na *exactly* hit."

7. Industrial Crafts

The Textile Industry

Think of Scottish industry, and whisky and wool must inevitably spring to mind as two of the largest and most important to the national economy. The fifty member companies of the Scottish Woollen Industry organisation which is concerned with the spinning of yarn and the weaving of cloth generate around £104,000,000 of business per annum. Double that to take account of the knitwear trade and the sum generated by non-members and the Harris Tweed trade, and the annual turnover rockets to well over the £200,000,000 mark.

The economic value of the textile trade to Scotland is high; but from a craft point of view, it is not just cash that counts, but quality – and quality has long been the hallmark of Scottish textiles. It has not always been so; before the widespread introduction of Cheviot sheep, the wool from the indigenous Borders and Highland sheep was of poor quality. The coarse cloth made from such wool always had a place in the market; almost every crofter knew how to spin and weave, and by the eighteenth century, the weaving of textiles as a cottage industry was well established.

The Industrial Revolution brought a change of emphasis, and the switch to power machinery was rapid. Spinning was the first craft skill to be mechanised. Mills had been established in Hawick and Galashiels in the Borders by the end of the eighteenth century. The hand-loom weaver's heyday was over by the early years of the nineteenth century. Weavers in the Borders were using flying-shuttle looms as early as 1788, carding machinery in 1790, and water-powered mills by 1800. The Borders in particular became a centre for spinning and weaving, and the demands of the new industry were matched by improvements in sheep-breeding techniques, and subsequently, more and better wool. It was a period of expansion, bringing work for thousands – weavers, dyers and fullers (who washed, stretched and beat the finished cloth).

The capacity of the fast-growing industry to supply cloth soon outstripped local demand, and an export trade rapidly grew. Scottish tweeds – the distinctive woollen fabric of mixed shades – became famous. In the Borders, as in some other parts of the country, tweeds were made in large, mechanised mills.

Elsewhere, such mechanisation was not practical and, especially in the Outer Hebrides, hand-woven cloth became a marketing bonus. The textile industry was not slow to diversify, and the import and spinning of cashmere, cotton, cambric and silk soon joined the established industries of wool-spinning and of tweed-weaving. Linen produced from flax grown in Scotland was a thriving industry for a period, and the highly skilled weavers around Paisley became renowned for their weaving of silks into the intricate Paisley shawls, at their most popular between 1820 and 1860. Tartan, which reached new heights of popularity when Queen Victoria showed her support for the style, was easier to produce using chemical dyes and industrial techniques than it had been on the old hand-looms, and the weaving

Opposite: Unglazed pots at Buchan's pottery at Crieff are stacked ready for decorating and firing.

(Della Matheson)

Below: Raw, de-haired cashmere in the wool store at the Kinross factory of Todd and Duncan.

(Todd and Duncan)

of tartan cloth has formed a staple part of the Border weaving trade for 100 years.

When or where knitting started, no-one is certain, but the 'original Tammy, the felted cap associated with the Scots, was knitted from the fifteenth century onwards and implied a long knowledge of the craft.'[1] It was as early as 1589 that the first knitting-frame was invented, by a Nottinghamshire clergyman called William Lee. It was designed to knit coarse woollen stockings. It was Englishmen, in fact, who established the knitting industry in Scotland.

In those early days, though the frame could work faster than any hand knitter, great skill was required from the operator, who needed superb co-ordination of hands and feet as well as considerable staying power. Keeping the thread even as it passed the needles, moving the bar of the frame while at the same time operating the treadles and watching every move of the thread, was exhausting work.[2]

For the whole of the Scottish textile industry, the coming of the railways meant expansion – greater import of wools and other raw materials, greater export of finished fabrics and garments. The experience of the weavers, the skill of the knitters, soon provided them with a market advantage, and 'Scottish' became synonymous with 'quality'. A change from hosiery to knitted outer garments was necessitated by the progress of fashion: as cotton and artificial silk, and later nylon, became standard for underwear the Border knitwear trade abandoned this area of the market and moved into the production of woollen outer wear, cardigans and jumpers. Fully fashioned garments, demanding skilful designing for machine-work, remained the province of the Scottish knitwear trade, again underlining the intention to stay at the 'quality' end of the market.

Although Scotland is known for sheep-farming, indigenous wools form less than 15 per cent of the raw material for knitwear and textile production, most of the wool being imported from Australasia and South Africa. 'Shetland' wool no longer comes exclusively from Shetland. Instead, it is a generic term describing a type of wool. Harris Tweed must, to earn its orb trade-mark, be woven from Scottish wool, and there are firms such as Hunters of Brora who still use wool which is primarily Scottish. Of the wool clipped from Scottish sheep, the coarse wool from the nine million Blackface which graze the hillsides goes largely to Italy to stuff mattresses, the balance going to the carpet trade. Concentration on quality has meant that Scottish firms have looked to lambswool, merino, angora and cashmere.

Cashmere is not, of course, wool, but hair from the cashmere goat which lives in remote parts of China, Mongolia, Afghanistan and Iran. The hair is not sheared; the soft under-hair is carefully combed by hand before embarking on its romantic voyage – 'the first step of the journey taking them across half the world, travelling on the backs of yaks and horses, rafts and sampans to trading stations where the fibre is baled and freighted to the processor.'[3] The biggest and longest established importer and spinner of cashmere in Scotland – indeed, in the Western hemisphere – is Todd and Duncan of Kinross south of Perth, part of Dawson International. The imported cashmere arrives at Dawson's mill in Bradford to be cleaned and dehaired. It is then sent to Kinross, where the long process of blending, dyeing and spinning begins. From

The spun cashmere on its cones is taken for final checking and packing.

(Todd and Duncan)

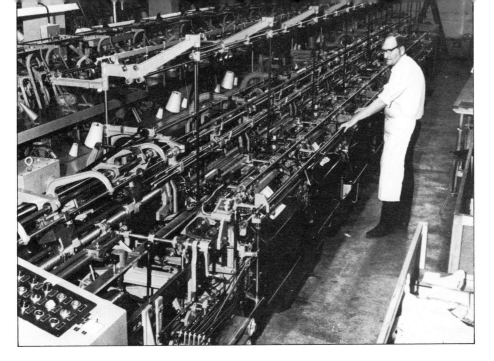

One-man operated electronically powered knitting machines are a far cry from the old wooden looms.

(Todd and Duncan)

here, the process more or less parallels that of wool-spinning.

The hair or wool is 'scoured' – that is, its oily content is removed – and water is sprayed on it to keep it under control and make it less electrostatic. From there it proceeds to huge dye-vats, where chemical dyes are applied. It is spin-dried and fed through drying machines, then packed firmly into large bales. The bales are weighed, then the blending process begins. Usually, the various wools are blended in huge bins, where various dye lots are brought together and mixed to achieve a large quantity of a uniform colour. The wool is then mixed with an emulsifying oil which allows the fibres to slip over each other in the carding machine.

The material is thrown into the carding-machines, where it is teased out over a series of rollers with fine pins. These straighten the fibres and present them in a uniform direction. The fine web of wool is then turned through 90 degrees to present in the opposite direction, where the process is repeated. Finally, the wool, now free from foreign matter and with the fibres lying in one direction, is separated into strands by a roller covered with rubber tapes, and is 'slubbed' – rubbed together through two large rubber rollers. At this stage the yarn is thread-like in appearance, but has no strength and would be unsuitable for weaving or knitting.

The strength comes through the spinning process. Mechanised since the end of the eighteenth century, spinning-mules today are highly sophisticated machines which feed the slubbed yarn through, spinning and stretching it on to spools at the required thickness. Breaks and knots are normally dealt with at a further stage, where a machine with electronically set parameters gauges the thickness of the wool and cuts and splices it where faults occur. For knitting, the wool is normally 'doubled' – spun a second time into a two-ply thickness.

At an ultra-modern mill such as Todd and Duncan's plant at Kinross, the latest technological innovations are utilised to ensure that the yarn is always top quality. Drying, for example, is by radio frequency, not steam, which treats the fibres more gently. Carding and spinning-machines are electronically controlled, knotting and splicing are automatic. Nevertheless, a worker from the old Alva Mill of 1867 would be able to walk into the Kinross mill today, and would understand exactly what was happening. The old spinning-jenny principle remains unchanged.

All Scottish spinners export a high percentage of their yarn, but some of it is passed forward to textile manufacturers in the Borders and elsewhere in Scotland. Industrial weaving employs exactly the same principles as hand-loom weaving, but the speed with which the operation is accomplished is considerable. The warp threads are set up on to a beam in the required length and pattern. This may be done by 'section warping', where one section of the warp pattern is set up and, once wound on to the beam, is moved across automatically to repeat the process, until the whole width is correctly warped. The beam is then carried to the loom, where the warp is threaded through

The oldest knitting machines looked like looms and were used by home workers.

the eyes of the shafts (there are at least four and as many as eighteen for complex designs) and slotted into the reed, which presses the weft thread into the cloth.

The design of power-looms varies. Some mills still have a number of flying-shuttle looms which, though slower than looms employing the bullet or rapier principle, require less time to warp up. These looms are, therefore, more economic for short lengths of cloth or for samples – although they demand greater skill to operate and may soon become obsolete. The woven cloth is checked over a light box in a mending room, where loose threads and knots are dealt with, then it goes

for scouring and milling – 'wet finishing'. In large washing-machines, the surplus dye and the oil is removed, leaving a soft cloth, pleasing to the touch. The milling process shrinks the cloth slightly, giving a fuller feel to the fabric. A centrifugal hydroextractor (spin-drier) takes most of the dampness out, then the cloth goes to a tentering-machine which dries the fabric and stretches it to the correct width. The jagged teeth on to which the cloth is fixed are the 'tenter-hooks'.

Finishing the cloth involves cropping off the excess surface hairs and pressing the cloth to set it and give it a fine finish. At every stage of spinning and weaving, quality controls are in operation to ensure that a high standard is maintained. This culminates in a final check against the standard – a master pattern which has been woven and submitted to the customer and accepted before the order is placed.

The craft element which remains an important part of the industrialised spinning and weaving processes is evident, too, in the knitting industry. One firm which retains a hand-work element in their output is Ballantyne's Sportswear of Innerleithen in the Borders (now also part of Dawson International). Here an important feature is the intarsia work, which is all hand done by highly skilled knitters. Working from an intricate colour chart pinned up in front of the frame, a knitter will take around two and a half hours to complete the front of a complex jumper. The knitting is carried out with the reverse side of the garment next to the knitter, and involves looping coloured threads by hand over a series of pins. Many patterns are traditional geometrics, while floral patterns – often knitted in two-ply wool on a one-ply background to give a raised effect – are popular, and animal designs are top favourite with the Japanese market.

Production of the sleeves and backs, skirts, cuffs and trimmings are carried out by machine; most are electronically controlled, and complex designs may be carried out through careful programming. At every stage of assembly, quality control is paramount, and checks are carried out on every garment, not just on a random sample. Assembling different parts of the garment, seaming, cutting and

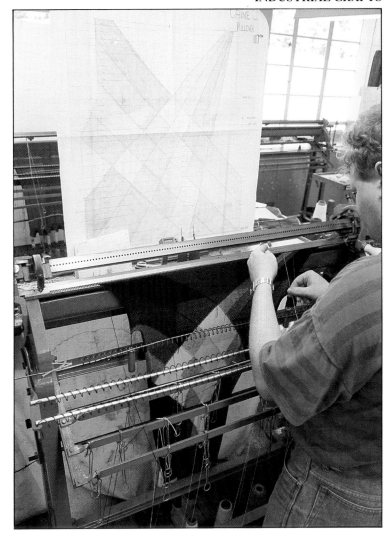

Above: complex intarsia designs are all hand knitted at Ballantyne's Sportswear in Innerleithen, in the Scottish Borders.

(Michael Siebert)

Left: quality control of intarsia cashmere sweaters is very important.

(Michael Siebert)

adding trims must be combined with a careful batch and order control to ensure that dye lots are not mixed. The finished garment goes to the millhouse, where washing rids the garment of the oily emulsion required for the knitting process. Quality garments require a 'loft' on the fibre, giving just the exact amount of milling to impart softness. Timing here is crucial, for this is a natural fibre which has been subjected to chemical processes. The time is different for every load – even different colours may require different treatment – and the attention of the millhouse workers is critical.

Finishing requires the stretching of the garments on frames to establish sizing, steam pressing to exact size and vacuuming to extract excess dampness. At this stage the knitted garment can be cut and treated in exactly the same way as woven cloth. The milling process causes the fibres to lock, and the stitches will not 'run' as in a hand-knitted garment. It can, therefore, be cut and shaped prior to adding neck trimmings and finishing touches. A final press is done in conjunction with a metre stick to check on size, and labelling and packing complete the long process.

The bulk of Scottish woollens go for export, particularly to the enormous American and Japanese markets. The skills which have been established here for centuries, and consolidated through periods of economic stability and recession, still thrive, keeping Scotland's name to the forefront in terms of quality woollen yarn, woven and knitted textiles. The determination of Scottish manufacturers to remain leaders in the woollen industry led to the establishment in 1909 of the Scottish Woollen Technical College (now the Scottish College of Textiles) in Galashiels in the Borders. Training in design and technical aspects, as well as research and technical innovation, are the industry's insurance policy for the preservation of skills for the future.

Lace Manufacture

The Irvine Valley in Central Scotland has been a centre of clothmaking since at least the sixteenth century, when Flemish and French Huguenot refugees brought their skills here with them. In 1566 Mary, Queen of Scots, extended the Royal Charter of 1491 and records show that the burgesses of Newmilns had 'full power and fair liberty of buying and selling wines, wax, woollen and linen cloths, broad and narrow, and other lawful merchandise.'

Newmilns and its neighbours Darvel and Galston had, by the middle of the eighteenth century, become hand-loom weaving towns. Like Harris in the Outer Hebrides, where every croft had its loom, each cottage in these small towns had a loom in the front room. The cloth, when finished, was carried on foot into Glasgow, a good 20 miles (32·18km) away, to be sold. It was not, though, lace that was woven on these hand-looms; the lace-making came later, in 1877, when power lace-looms were introduced by Messrs Hood, Morton, Cleland and Co. The growth of the lace industry saw the decline of hand-loom weaving, but it brought prosperity to these Ayrshire towns. The fortunes of the industry have fluctuated, but order books today are full, and the machines run night and day.

Traditionally, Scottish lace was woven in two-tone cotton, although modern laces carry a small element of nylon, making it stronger and easier to care for. The term 'woven' here is a misnomer, for lace is 'twisted' rather than woven.

Work starts in the design room, where new designs, as big as 90in (2·286m) long by 60in (1·829m) wide, are hand-painted and laminated, ready for submission to the client for approval. It is painstaking work, and the drawing up of a pattern and its translation into a design for the Jacquard-punch can take six months or more. Patterns have changed little over the years – contemporary designs have been attempted from time to time, but the old favourites of birds, bows and baskets seem to work best and find greatest approval. Very often the designer's task is to translate the rough ideas of the client into a workable form, or to match in lace a sample of wall-paper or upholstery fabric. The visualised pattern is transferred to graph paper and keyed in red (for solid cloth), green (for finer effect), or white (representing holes in the lace).

When the pattern has been drafted, it goes to the card-cutter, who hand-punches holes into the cards which give the machines the information they need to weave the lace.

The cotton used to come into the factory in hanks; now it comes in 'cheeses' and is in the form of single yarn. This must be twisted and spun on doubling-machines to make it the quality and strength required for the lace-machines. The bobbin-stripper is responsible for ensuring that the slender bobbins which move backward and forward through the yarn, twisting and catching the cotton into place, are filled and tensioned correctly. There are various different gauges of lace; at the biggest

Many of the industrial lace machines used at Newmilns are over 100 years old.

(Michael Siebert)

lace factory in Britain, Johnston, Shields and Co. Ltd at Newmilns, four gauges are still made: the coarsest is four point (with four bobbins to the inch), varying through eight point, and ten point up to twelve point (with twelve bobbins to the inch). Each bobbin is wound with nylon yarn for strength, and carries about 150yds (137·16m) of thread. At Johnston Shields, the machines make cloth 360in (9·144m) long; on a twelve-point gauge, therefore, there would be more than four thousand bobbins at work.

The spooler ties the spools of yarn on at the back of the machine, and the responsibility of the lace making passes to the weaver, who is in charge of the machine. The pattern of the lace is dictated by the Jacquard-cards which feed through the Jacquard high above the lace-machine. There may be as many as 150 cards for one repeat. The cards feed through on a single belt to allow uninterrupted weaving, and it takes only a matter of minutes to change them for a new pattern. Once weaving is ready to start, it is simply a matter of keeping an eye on the machines to ensure that none of the threads is broken and that all the yarns are running freely. The Jacquard, spools and bobbins do the rest.

A wire roller called a 'porcupine' controls the cloth, winding it into a roll between 30 and 50yds (27·432 and 45·72m) in length. Once cut off the machine, the cloth goes for washing and finishing. Lace may be cut into circles for table-cloths and hemmed, attached on to the bottom of net curtains, ruched and made up into blinds or simply rolled into bales and packed for despatch. The output is prodigious and varied – from traditional Scottish lace to yashmaks for the Arab world (made by the thousand, every week).

The lace-machines are large and impressive; they are also durable. Some machines at the Johnston Shields factory are more than 100 years old. It is not that times have not changed – ultra-modern machinery produces nylon or polyester lace, using an automated process which is in reality more akin to knitting than weaving. The fact is quite simply that in the case of traditional Scottish lace, the old ways are the best.

Glass Manufacture

By the middle of the seventeenth century glass-making was firmly established at Leith,

Portobello and Prestonpans on the outskirts of Edinburgh – to meet 'a large local demand for bottles and drinking glasses needed for imported wine and locally-made whisky and ale.'[4] The industry filled the demand for sound, basic goods, but always suffered from competition from foreign imports.

Historically, the most famous Scottish glass is the Jacobite glass made during the Jacobite risings of 1715 and 1745. Glasses inscribed with symbols of Jacobite loyalty – at first overt, later secret – were used by Jacobite sympathisers to show their support for the cause. Symbols included the rose for the English Crown, with either one bud or two to symbolise the Old or Young Pretender. The thistle for the Scottish crown is rare; the oak leaf stands for the restoration of the Stuart dynasty. Forget-me-nots, daffodils and carnations all have their hidden meanings, as do the star, jay (standing for James), compass and caterpillars.

Despite their popularity – and now their extreme collectability – many of these glasses were not Scottish at all, but were made in Newcastle-upon-Tyne, although many may have been engraved in Edinburgh.

Around the time of the popularity of these glasses, a new Edinburgh glass factory was born, and by the end of the eighteenth century, there were at least six glass works based in Leith. It was a period when the drinking of

claret had become fashionable, and wineglasses of a good quality were much in demand. In 1792 a contributor to *The Bee*, a periodical, commented that about four years earlier, the Glass House Company of Leith 'began to manufacture white glass, they fell into the way of cutting it or ornament and engraving upon it. In this last department they have reached a higher degree of perfection than it has perhaps anywhere else ever obtained.'[5]

Glass manufacture in Leith, and the neighbouring town of Portobello, suffered a steady

Above: advertisement for the 'Thistle' service.

(Edinburgh Crystal)

Left: glass engraving at Edinburgh Crystal takes four years to learn.

(Edinburgh Crystal)

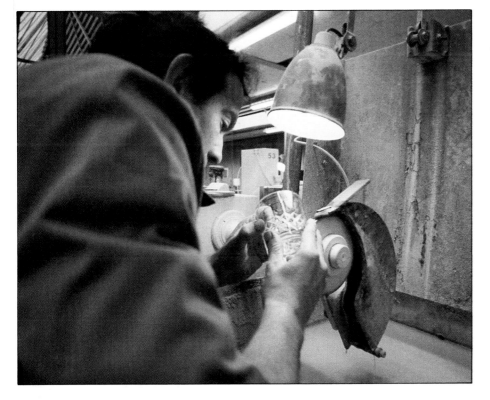

Opposite: engraved Edinburgh Crystal vase by Norman Orr.
(Ken Wilson)

Right: industrial glassmaking is very much a team operation.
(Edinburgh Crystal)

decline as the industry took hold in Edinburgh itself; and the tradition set in the late eighteenth century was sustained and is now well upheld by the sole survivor of all the old firms, the Edinburgh Crystal Glass Co.

Edinburgh Crystal's works were originally in Leith Walk. Alexander Jenkinson's Leith Walk Glass Works excited praise for the quality of its ware. In an 1875 edition of the *Art Journal* the director of the Edinburgh Museum, Professor Archer, wrote,

> . . . in the Paris exhibition of 1867 the French reporters of the jury wrote in terms of great praise of the engraving and exquisite clearness of the material in the specimens of ornamental flint-glass from Edinburgh . . . it is quite certain that the admiration excited by their productions has had great effect in stimulating both masters and artisans, and causing a very considerable development of the manufacture both in Edinburgh and Glasgow.[6]

'Flint-glass' was once made from silica flints, ground and calcined, then heated with soda and lime or potash.

It was in the 1880s that the crystal glass for which the company has become famous was developed. Crystal is so named because it emulates 'rock crystal', a natural semi-precious stone. Today's crystal is made from the pure white sand found at Lochaline in the West of Scotland. The sand is put through a magnet to extract the excess iron. Potash is added to help it to fuse and to eliminate air, and 36 per cent red oxide gives weight and brilliance. Breakages in the factory are also recycled, and the 'cullet' helps to reduce the melting point of the glass in the furnaces.

The Edinburgh Crystal factory, now at Penicuik near Edinburgh, is one of the largest and most modern glass factories in Europe: there are sixteen furnaces, most of them in constant use. Glass is loaded into the furnaces at night, each one holding 15¾cwt (around 800kg), and production takes place during the day.

During the melting cycle, the furnaces will run at 1400 degrees centigrade; for working, the temperature will be reduced to between 1080 and 1150 degrees depending on the type of article being produced. Working in teams of three or four, the workers in the glass factory will make something over 200 glasses every day. In a wine-glass team, the 'footmaker'

draws the glass from the furnace and blows it into a mould. The 'servitor' 'casts on' the glass for the stem and foot, while the 'bit gatherer' provides him with the glass for the stem and carries the excess glass back to the furnace. It is a skilled and intricate process, and the apprenticeship period is five or six years. Some boys never get the knack of working with glass, while others slot into a team and never leave it. The glassworker's tools are unashamedly old-fashioned – the blow-iron for blowing, the steel slab called a marver on which the glass is rolled to give it its preliminary shape and a cooler skin to contain the bubble, calipers to check dimensions, wooden blocks for shaping and spring steel tools (pucellas) for preshaping the stems. Once complete, the glass is carried to a lehr for the final annealing process of long, slow cooling.

In the Process Department the excess blown glass is scored by an industrial diamond, heated slightly, and 'cracked off'. The rim, which is very sharp, is ground on to carborundum pads, sometimes bevelled by an automatic process, sometimes melted slightly. In the Marking Room, guide lines are painted on for the cutters. With a dozen or more basic production lines, each with an intricate set of patterns, the cutter has to have a good memory, and will serve a four-year apprenticeship. The glass is cut on wheels impregnated with

diamond dust, or rough and smooth cut with carborundum and fine carbon. Great care is needed to ensure that exactly the right pressure is applied.

The cut glass is washed in detergent, in a large sink through which ultrasonic waves are passed to agitate the water. This removes dust and the guide lines. It is then put into Monel metal baskets (an alloy of mainly nickel with some copper) and taken to an acid bath which smooths the cut edges and gives the glass added brilliance. Care is needed in the timing of the operation, as the acid physically eats away the glass. It is then, finally, rinsed and dried by hand.

At Edinburgh Crystal, the intricate cut work is often complemented by sand-etched or hand-engraved designs. For sand-etching, transfers are made by silk-screen on tissue paper, and sand is blasted at high speed to etch away the exposed surfaces of the glass. It is a considerably simpler and less skilled operation than hand-engraving, which is done on copper wheels lubricated with an abrasive oil. The engraving of these glasses requires judgement, dexterity and artistic awareness, and engravers spend at least four years learning their skills.

A final meticulous inspection process ensures that no crystal leaves the factory unless it achieves the correct standards.

It is worth noting here that Scotland's fine contemporary copper-wheel engravers owe their heritage to Edinburgh Crystal's predecessors, the Ford Company of Leith. Ford employed a number of engravers in the late nineteenth century, notably the Bohemians by name of Müller (which they changed to Miller). Their work was of a high standard and attracted widespread praise. In the 1940s a lady called Helen Munro Turner, influenced by the engraving of Edinburgh Crystal (for whom she did some work), went to Germany to study under Professor von Eiff, and returned to open the Glass Department at Edinburgh College of Art. Her work, and the work of her students, was far in advance of anything happening in England at the time – almost all engraving there was diamond-point. Many of Scotland's leading glass workers and engravers were taught by Mrs Turner – among them Alison Geissler, David Gullane, Denis Mann and Colin Terris (the latter two now working for Caithness Glass at Caithness and Perth respectively).

Caithness Glass, established in 1960, produces distinctive heavy coloured and engraved glass, and paper-weights. The company opened its first factory in Wick in the north of

'Blocking' – one technique used in making a paperweight to shape the weight.

(Caithness Glass plc)

Scotland as a bid to counter the rising unemployment caused by the decline of the traditional industries of fishing and farming. Their engraving shop opened in 1968, and is now one of the largest in Europe. Success bred success, and the company opened further factories in Oban on the west coast and in Perth.

Paperweights

While the craft of glass-making in Scotland goes back at least to the seventeenth century, the contemporary forte – the making of paperweights – has only a short history. Salvador Ysart, a Spaniard, came with his family to Scotland via France around 1915. He was a glass-blower by trade, and his skills were well used by the Leith Flint Glassworks in Edinburgh, makers of Edinburgh Crystal. In 1922 Ysart moved to the Perth firm, Moncrieff's Glassworks, where he developed a range of Art Deco coloured ware named 'Monart' glass.

But it was Paul Ysart, Salvador's son, who was particularly interested in making paperweights, and who applied his skills to experimental work with millefiori canes and lamp-worked flowers and birds. It seems that he had no knowledge of the famous French factories, Baccarat of Saint Louis and Clichy, which made weights in quantity during the middle of the nineteenth century.

Paper-weights remained very much a sideline, however, until Stuart Drysdale, who had been managing Vasart (the successor to Monart) and then Strathearn Glass, set up his own company, Perthshire Paperweights. Drysdale had seen an article in an American magazine *Woman's Day* published in 1965 on the Bergstrom Art Center and Museum collection of antique French paper-weights. It was a revelation; the craftsmen were consulted, resolutions were made, and a new determination to do as well, and better, was born. Since then, Perthshire Paperweights have joined the very select band of manufacturers around the world whose artefacts are

The colourful and intricate millefiori work is an old craft. Though not particularly Scottish, it has been taken up by Scottish firms in a big way.
(Perthshire Paperweights)

considered highly collectable.

Perthshire Paperweights specialise in millefiori work with multi-coloured glass rods, cut and arranged into intricate patterns. The first stage is to make the canes, by gathering glass, rolling it in a coloured powder, and pressing it into a mould. The process is repeated several times to build up colours and patterns within the cane. At this stage the cane is around 3in (7·6cm) in diameter and 6in (15·2cm) long. It is then heated again, held at both ends on pontil rods, and stretched to as much as 20ft (6·096m). Twisted spirals are made by attaching one end of the cane to a cranking device which is slowly turned as the second craftsman walks away. As the cane stretches, the design is miniaturised. Many canes can be fused into one to make even more complex designs. Great care is taken in the cane-making process, but much of each length is too uneven to be used.

Using a variety of canes, the weight is made up by assembling small lengths on to an iron template with tweezers. Any one worker may assemble from ten to thirty designs a day. The template is heated and placed inside a circular collar, while a gather of molten glass is drawn from the furnace and the two elements are fused. The relative temperatures are critical. The clear crown is then carefully shaped, the weight is knocked off the rod into a sand-box, and carried to the furnace for the final annealing process. At any stage in the procedure the weight may be abandoned, and final scrutiny is critical – only 30 per cent of the weights started make it to the show-case.

Pottery

Pottery did not develop as an industry in Scotland until well after Union with England in the eighteenth century. Then production took a sudden upswing, and Scottish potteries began really to come into their own:

> Pottery making tended to gravitate towards those areas which could supply its basic needs: clay to make the pots, and coal to fire them; sufficient labour not only to man the factories but also possessing the aptitude to learn new skills; a ready means of transporting the finished ware in bulk, which in those days meant going by sea, coupled with a proximity to population centres and the markets which they could provide.[7]

Two areas with these essentials for production began to emerge naturally: Glasgow, and a string of small villages along the East Lothian coast, east of Edinburgh. Skilled labour was imported from England, and experiments in types of ware and kinds of clay began. By the end of the century, production was well established, and the foundations laid down for a thriving industry in the nineteenth century.

The Britannia Pottery, Glasgow, around 1900, giving a clear impression of the scale of its output.

(*Britain at Work*, an anonymous book published 1902)

The goods produced by the Scottish factories were varied. In Glasgow, 'Nautilus' porcelain was produced at the Possil Factory, while Bell's Pottery produced unglazed parian ware (an unglazed porcelain which looked like marble) and high quality bone china. The Glasgow Verreville factory also produced china, while in the east, porcelain was produced at Castle Pottery in Prestonpans. Also at Prestonpans the original Cadell factory produced white salt-glazed stoneware, although the east coast potteries were largely famed for their creamware. Fundamental to the success of the industry was the everyday table-ware made from earthenware, usually decorated by the application of transfers. Even easier to apply was sponge printing, where a simple decoration was dabbed on by a sponge which had been cut to shape. Spongeware became identifiable as distinctively Scottish.

Perhaps the most commercial product of all was the stoneware manufactured in huge quantities by a number of the Glasgow factories and by Buchan and Gray of Edinburgh – whisky flagons, jars for storing everything from oatmeal to cream, from beer to blacking, ink bottles, cream jugs, hot-water bottles, jugs and vases.

While the production of pottery became big business for Scotland – with potteries not just in East Lothian and Glasgow, but also in Kirkcaldy, Alloa, Aberdeen, Errol, Montrose, Cumnock, Barrhead (where heavy fire-clay was made for pipes and sanitary ware by the Victorian Pottery of Douglas Shanks) – the tradition of hand-thrown production on a small scale did not entirely disappear. In Lewis and elsewhere in the Western Isles, 'croggan ware' was produced: 'This primitive ware was hand-made without the wheel, glazed with nothing more than milk and fired in a clamp kiln of turf and seaweed. It provides the intriguing possibility of a continuous tradition of pottery making in the Hebrides stretching from the late bronze age into the twentieth century.'[8]

At its height, the Scottish pottery industry was both prolific and famous. A vast export trade sprang up; the Cadell pottery exported its ware to 53 ports around the world during the late eighteenth century, with the East and West Indies and America being prime markets. In the nineteenth century, success continued through the prestigious international trade fairs. One firm, Bailey's of Alloa, claimed that their tea-pots were so popular that 'to cater for demand they kept 100 000 tea-pots in stock at all times, which was

reputedly less than one month's production.'[9]

The pottery industry in Scotland had a short life, however; for 150 years it thrived, but increasing competition from Staffordshire and elsewhere in Europe, changes in demand and the loss of overseas markets brought about by the First World War all contributed to the decline of a once booming industry. By the middle of this century, almost all of the big potteries had gone, and now just one survives.

Buchan's of Portobello, dating from 1867 though based then in a factory of 1770, was at one time one of Scotland's largest manufacturers. The Portobello pottery closed in 1972, but moved to Crieff in Perthshire, where it continues production of its distinctive 'Thistle' ware among other lines.

John Clarkson has been working as a potter for fifty years, and still throws for Buchan's at Crieff.

(Della Matheson)

The huge flagons standing some 3ft (91·4cm) off the ground which were once a common item on Buchan's stock-list, are now no more than a memory in their archive store. 'We couldn't possibly produce them now,' says Alexander Reay, their production manager. 'They would be totally uneconomic, unsuited to firing in modern kilns, and wastage would be too high – and besides, there are too many cheap imports from the Far East to contend with.' Flagons for whisky, by contrast, have been made since at least the turn of the century, and are still made to order for the large whisky distillers.

Buchan's, though factory-based in its production methods, retain a large element of handcrafting in their procedures. Most of the pots are hand-painted, and at least 35 per cent are still hand-thrown. John Clarkson has been a thrower for 50 years, and well remembers the 'gas mantle overhead, and wheels driven from a main shaft. Clay production was much simpler – we simply had a square bath filled with raw clay, added water, and put it through the pug-mill.'

Today's clay production is very much more sophisticated. Stoneware ball clays are mixed with a small percentage of china clay to lighten the colour, and feldspar, which acts as a flux, helping the clay to vitrify. The mixture is fed through a blunger, sieved via magnets which extract the excess iron, and mixed with water to a liquid form, slip. The mixture is stirred slowly to get out the air, pumped via a filter press to get the water out until it is just the right consistency. It is then fed through a de-airing pug-mill and left for ten days on pallets to 'mature'.

At Buchan's, the range of shapes is either made on a jolley and jigger, slipcast in pre-formed moulds, or hand-thrown. 'Hand-throwing may seem uneconomic because it is labour intensive, but many customers prefer the end result. The pots are heavier and have distinctive characteristics. Besides, it would be impossible for us to store enough moulds to cover the entire range by slipcasting.'

The pots, shaped and 'fettled' to get rid of mould marks, are dried, then spray glazed and hand-painted. At Buchan's, the most distinctive range are the 'Thistle' pots, although other ranges are produced, including the nostalgic 'Country Cottage' brown and white earthenware made half a century ago and now finding a new lease of life.

Buchan's is one of Scotland's largest potteries, and is certainly the oldest still in existence. The other potteries of any size are the Larbert Pottery near Falkirk, Dunoon Ceramics near Glasgow and Highland Stoneware at Lochinver on the north-west coast – all very successful, and all with their own distinctive ranges. None compares in scale, though, with the potteries for which Scotland was so famous in the late eighteenth and nineteenth centuries.

While the industrial potteries fell by the wayside, one by one, so the individual craft potters began to emerge. The sixties, when

An important hand craft element is the decoration of the 'Thistle' pots for which Buchan's is so famous.
(Della Matheson)

handmade goods began to be prized, was also a time when many potters fled the 'rat-race' and set up in business, making domestic ware in a small way. Some craft potters developed great expertise, and gained substantial reputations as ceramists. Early experiments with form, glaze, and decoration were consolidated in the eighties, and the enormous range of work now available in Scotland is tribute to these pioneers. Sgraffito, slip-trailing, raku-firing, lustre-glazing are all to be found, while ancient techniques are not completely abandoned. Some potters still practise wood-firing and salt-glazing, though the old technique of sponge decoration appears to be all but lost.

The days of mass production on a huge scale may have gone; but the age-old tradition of pottery production in Scotland is alive and thriving.

Cooperage

Barrel-making is one of the very oldest of crafts – and not one that could ever be undertaken by the amateur. The building of a wood container that is strong, hardwearing and watertight demands strength and skill, sleight of hand and a keen eye.

Wooden casks were once used for holding everything from flour to gunpowder, from beer and brandy to butter. Many industries used cooper-made vessels in dyeing, distilling, brewing, mining, metal-work and glass manufacturing processes. Casks were made to hold a range of products from soap and syrup to fish. In 1913 the herring trade alone employed 1500 coopers.

Coopers specialised in 'wet', 'dry' or 'white' work. Dry coopers made casks with bulging sides to hold dry goods. The white cooper made straight-sided vessels such as buckets or tubs. The most skilled of all was the wet cooper, who made casks to hold liquids, notably beer and spirits.

No trade has, perhaps, dwindled so completely and so suddenly as coopering. Mass production of metal and plastic containers, together with the increasing cost of quality timber and the labour-intensive nature of coopering, has to a large extent made the old-fashioned wooden cask redundant. The one exception is the wine-making and distilling trades; oak casks are ideal for maturing strong spirits, the flavour imparted is impossible to imitate by any other means. Only in Spain, America and in Scotland, therefore, does coopering still exist on any scale. Even so, 'We don't make barrels here any more. It's not economic,' explained Harry Woods, manager of one commercial cooperage in the west of

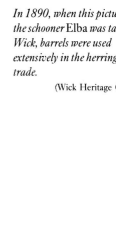

In 1890, when this picture of the schooner Elba *was taken at Wick, barrels were used extensively in the herring trade.*

(Wick Heritage Centre)

Scotland. 'Under American law, containers may be used only once. So it's much cheaper to import American surplus. There are perhaps 200 coopers in the whole of Scotland. We used to employ 21 coopers at the Kelvin Cooperage. Now there are only four of us, and we are concerned only with repair work.' Three to four thousand barrels a month still pass through the cooperage for checking and repair. Occasionally barrels will be knocked down and remade, with perhaps a new bung stave (the weakest part) replaced.

The craft is a picturesque one, with a language all its own. Each size of cask has its own name – butts (the largest), puncheons, hogsheads, barrels, firkins. There are even regional variants for the names given to some of the tools and processes. Traditionally the oak was 'quarter sawn' – cut along the length of the tree into half, then again into quarters. These quarters were then cut diagonally across the medullary rays (the rings); cut in this fashion, the wood was impervious and resisted warping. The staves were seasoned for as long as five years before they reached the cooper's workshop to be 'dressed' (shaped by axe and a series of curved and straight knives) then bevelled using a 'jointer'. This operation demands great skill, as the shape of the staves is critical for a tight fit.

A barrel begins to take shape when the cooper 'raises' it inside a retaining hoop (the raising hoop) balanced against the stomach. Once assembled, a second hoop is dropped over to give strength to the centre of the barrel. The staves are straightened at the top by eye, using a mallet to tap them level. The barrel is leaned against the working block and the inside of the top is 'chimed' (bevelled) using a 'crumb-knife' to allow the end to be slipped in. A 'croze' – usually a home-made tool – is used to cut a channel inside the top into which the end will be seated.

Part of the cooper's job is to make sure that the cask will have the correct capacity. After the first groove has been cut, the cask is turned over and measured carefully before the second groove is cut, to make any adjustments necessary. Finished hoops are now fitted to replace the working ones. The metal is measured and riveted, then the cask is measured and chalked to show the correct site for the final hoop.

The end or 'head' of the barrel is made from several planks – usually three to five – which are pinned together with dowels and sealed with flags (reeds), a natural material which is still the most effective form of gasket. The head is not completely circular, but is cut slightly larger at the cants (the end-planks), because the head squeezes in over the years, but always with the grain, never against it. Once it has been cut to size, the head is 'cut in' with a heading knife – that is, it is bevelled to provide a sharp ridge which slips down into the groove of the barrel. The head is slipped into the cask by taking off the chime hoop, opening the joints slightly, packing the groove with reed to form a seal, and tapping the head into position with a hammer. The staves are closed up and the chime hoop hammered back. The joints in the head run towards the bung-hole, so that its strength runs the right way – the cask usually being stored with the bung up. A tension iron forces the flag into place, and the joints at the top of the cask are eased to allow a sliver of flag to be slipped in before the chime hoop is slipped back. The second head is inserted using a heading vice to help to pull the head into place.

The completed cask is 'dressed' with a 'plucker' (the west of Scotland term) or a 'buzz'. This is to scrape the outside of the cask to smooth out any rough joints. The hoops are hammered home (today this is normally done on a machine, saving some of the most backbreaking of the cooper's work), and the bung-hole bored. Finally, it must be tested by an air and water pressure gauge.

Few coopers now make casks in Britain, and imported ones are ready-charred inside, to add flavour to the maturing spirit and reduce porosity. Some distillers maintain that the charring becomes less effective after a few uses, and the charring is repeated – but in the modern fashion, over gas jets. Apprentices are seldom taken on in the coopering trade and this industry, already in a severe decline, will face a crisis when its experienced craftsmen retire.

Opposite: Harry Woods of Kelvin Cooperage assembling the barrel into the top hoop (top left); making the rim inside the barrel for the lid, using a chiv (top right); constructing one of the hoops (bottom left), and dressing the barrel with a plucker to smooth out rough joints (bottom right).

(Andrea Cringean)

1. Jackie Moore, *Rich and Rare, The Story of Dawson International*, Henry Melland, London 1986, p. 20.
2. *Ibid.*, p. 27.
3. *Ibid.*, p. 30.
4. H. W. Woodward, *The Story of Edinburgh Crystal*, Dema Glass Ltd, Edinburgh 1984, p. 1.
5. *Ibid.*, p. 8.
6. *Ibid.*, p. 21.
7. Graeme Cruickshank, *Scottish Pottery*, Shire Publications Ltd, 1987, p. 5.
8. *Ibid.*, p. 23.
9. *Ibid.*, p. 24.

8. Craft in Architecture

The divorce of 'craft' and 'architecture' is a modern phenomenon. In centuries past no distinction was made between the two: both married in the process of converting design into structure. Country mansions, royal palaces, churches and memorials all bear testament to the skills of wood- and stone-carvers, blacksmiths, ornamental plasterers and artists in stained glass. Such craftsmen worked with the country's best-known architects to great effect.

Sir Robert Lorimer, who left Edinburgh University in 1884 to take up articles with the architect, Hew Wardrop, was said to be quite possessive about the craftsmen he employed. Lorimer's attitude to craft in architecture was strongly influenced by the Arts and Crafts Movement (which elevated the traditional work of the tradesmen to art) and in particular by George Frederic Bodley, one of the leading architects of the Movement. Bodley viewed every building as a work of art democratically fashioned by a group of craftsmen, of whom the architect was but one.

Lorimer used a number of craftsmen and firms regularly in his Scottish buildings. The plaster ceilings in his country homes, which usually derived from historical examples, were modelled with the help of a man called Beattie. The former Edinburgh firm of Scott Morton, who in 1905 had enough work to be able to employ 60 wood-carvers, did most of Lorimer's joinery and architectural woodwork. For the fine wood-carving of the Thistle Chapel in St Giles' Cathedral, Edinburgh, a work begun in 1909, Lorimer employed the talents of the Clow brothers who lived in Hanover Street – two legendary craftsmen affectionately dubbed Tweedledum and Tweedledee, who would spend their holidays in Belgium studying the work of that country's famous wood-carvers. Lorimer also used the services of the craftsman in wrought-iron: in fact, one of his first designs in wrought-iron was a well-head arch at Earlshall, Fife, a simple twisted bar surmounted by a large flower which resembles the flower in the old gates at Traquair House, Peebleshire.

Another Scottish architect renowned for treating craft and design as an integral part of building was Charles Rennie Mackintosh. Wrought-iron was used frequently in the fabric of his architecture – usually in a way which was functional as well as ornamental. The gates to Glasgow School of Art, which is perhaps Mackintosh's best-known creation, are part of the Art Nouveau entrance to the building, and the decorative iron brackets to the studio windows were designed to support the window-cleaner's planks. They are, as one writer commented, '. . . the most discussed window brackets in history.'[1] Wrought-iron was also used profusely in the famous Willow Tearooms, Glasgow, both on the façade and in the interior, where an elaborate balustrade was an important element in the overall design.

The involvement of decorative craftsmen by architects like Lorimer and Mackintosh, and indeed by centuries of builders before them, is not a practice that has continued at the same level into the 1980s. The age-old dialogue between architect and artisan has been superseded by modern building methods. No longer is the craftsman's work necessary to the construction of the building. The tendency nowadays is to use craft in new architecture as an afterthought. That is despite the support of the concept of craft in architecture by such groups as the Saltire Society, who since the 1970s have been making Art in Architecture Awards. Many of their awards over the years have been in the area of 'moveable' as opposed to integrated craft – tapestries, for example, rather than stained glass or carved stone.

While commissions to craftsmen for new buildings may not be plentiful, there is still one area where their services are continually in demand. This is in the field of conservation. The support and encouragement of certain traditional skills by groups like the Edinburgh New Town Conservation Committee, and the Conservation Bureau started by the Scottish Development Agency, has perhaps prevented the demise of some traditional architectural crafts. The National Trust for Scotland has also played an important role in continuing the tradition of patronage to craft specialists. The restoration work instigated by the Trust on one of its newer properties, Fyvie Castle in Aberdeenshire, took what was described as an 'army' of craftsmen to complete. In addition to building specialists like masons, slaters, plumbers, blacksmiths and electricians, the Trust employed fine art restorers, upholsterers and decorators, even a gunsmith to restore the Castle's large collection of weapons and armour.

Opposite: blue fish window by John Clark in the Cafe Gandolfi, Glasgow.

(John Clark)

Brian Robertson still practises the skills he learned in one of Edinburgh's famous wood-working firms.

Carving

Wood-carving

Some of the oldest Scottish examples of carving in wood and stone can be seen in the National Museums of Scotland in Queen Street, Edinburgh. A small wooden box carved with Celtic patterns lays claim to being the oldest extant piece of woodwork: it dates from before the tenth century AD and was discovered in a bog on a farm in Orkney in 1885. The Museum's ornamental carving from early sixteenth-century interiors gives a better idea of a craft that is now almost extinct. The Montrose Panels, with their pattern of thistles, roses, oak sprays, and birds, are believed to have come from a hospital, while the carved oak Seton panels, which show a griffin, thistles and a pierced heart, are reputed to have come from an East Lothian church. Other existing wood-carving from about the same period are the Stirling Heads, carved to decorate the ceiling of the King's Presence Chamber within the palace at Stirling Castle. Carved during the short period of Scottish Renaissance art, the oak medallions portray a number of court figures as well as historical, Biblical and mythical personages. About a quarter of the original set of 56 heads is missing, and the quality of the existing medallions suggests that at least two carvers worked on the heads. The identities of the carvers can only be supposed and, in fact, one might have French: James V, who built the palace before his death in 1542, imported French craftsmen to help with this work.

Requests for the type of architectural wood-carving described above are rare nowadays. One wood-carver still practising in the field, albeit part-time, is Brian Robertson of Edinburgh, who did his apprenticeship with Scott Morton, the firm used by Lorimer. He worked on ecclesiastical commissions like the reredos screen for St Michael's in Linlithgow near Edinburgh, a project which took Robertson and two other carvers just over a year to execute. From Scott Morton, he went to Charles Henshaw and Sons, architectural metal-workers, where his carving abilities were used for another purpose – to make models for casting.

Heraldic carving and lettering are another part of the Scottish wood-carving tradition. This craft flourished at the end of World War II, when commemorative plaques, either in bronze or in wood, were much in demand. Robertson claims to have more than a nodding acquaintance with every bronze plaque in George Street, Edinburgh: during his spell with Henshaw's he carved numerous letter panels and coats of arms for translation into bronze. Not that he finds this low-relief carving much of a challenge. 'There are no real skills needed to carve letters' he maintains. 'Personally I like to work on something more decorative.' One commission which gave him the required satisfaction was a carving of

the four evangelists for St Cuthbert's Church, Melrose in the Borders.

Stone-carving

Stone-carving was also once a highly specialised craft. Scotland's natural resources provided an ample supply, not only for the fabric of buildings but also for the carver's hammer and chisel. Aberdeen granite is well known, and so, too, is the contribution made by Craigleith Quarry in Edinburgh: some of the

Dry construction of spire in Ian Ketchin's Wallyford workshop.

(Della Matheson)

finest quality sandstone ever quarried went from Craigleith into the Georgian buildings of the New Town and to London. But there were other native stones that also achieved distinction: Caithness paving slabs at the turn of the century were shipped regularly from Thurso in the north of Scotland, to Australia, America and South Africa; for rooftops blue/grey Ballachulish slate sparkling with pyrites (that industry in the late 1800s employed nearly 600 men); highly polished Portsoy marble for ornaments, and so on. Stone is endless in its variety.

Some of the oldest examples of the stone-carver's craft can be found in the sculpted and inscribed stones in the collection of the National Museums of Scotland in Queen Street, Edinburgh. Primitive figures in relief, incised crosses, and Celtic designs feature in the work of carvers of an earlier age. Today, the work of the country's stone-carvers is more apt to be found in the use of environmental art in architecture or in the restoration of churches and public buildings.

There are sculptors like Jake Kempsall, who made the stone mural for the new Glasgow Sheriff Court – a mural in Hoptonwood limestone some 10ft (3·048m) in length depicting aspects of Glasgow as well as justice – and Frances Pelly who likes the tradition of stone, but uses it in an unconventional way. They are more artists than craftsmen in the tradition of the carvers who once learned their skills from masters. A very few stone-carvers follow a different path – their skills are used for decorative architectural detail.

Although there is limited demand for the stone-carver in Scotland, one mammoth job of restoration has called upon the skills of many stone experts, including the carver: the renovation of the Victorian-built National Portrait Gallery in Queen Street, Edinburgh. The red sandstone used in the building's construction came from Dumfriesshire over 100 years ago and the quarry that produced the original stone has been reopened for the supply of compatible material. The work on the crumbling face of the gallery, which has suffered badly from weathering, has been going on for some time and as funds permit. One carver, Ian Ketchin, started working on components of replacement spires and balustrading in 1982.

Ketchin has a workshop on Wallyford Industrial Estate near Musselburgh outside Edinburgh and he carves in either wood or stone, though latterly most of his work has been in stone. One of his first commissions in

stone was a replacement cherub for Cammo House, Corstorphine in Edinburgh. Later he carved a replacement 'caryatid mullion' (pillar or column head) for the Caledonian Hotel at the west end of Princes Street and handrail terminations for the stone staircase to the undercroft in St Giles' Cathedral. He has also done replacement work on the Victorian Gothic architecture of St Paul's Cathedral, Dundee.

Plaster-work

Another old craft which has found new life in restoration is that of ornamental plaster-work. 'Plaster of Paris' made from gypsum deposits under Montmartre, first came to Britain in the thirteenth century. But the most frequently used plaster in the following centuries was a mixture of lime ('slaked' with water to reduce the caustic quality), sand and hair – from cows, bullocks or, for finer work, goats. One Robert Greenhorn, a tanner, was paid 6s 8d (33p) per stone of 'common hair' in 1674 for plaster-work then being undertaken at Holyroodhouse.[2] Hair, it is said, was added to the mixture of lime and sand at the rate of 1 to 2lb (·45–·91kg) of hair for each 2 to 3 cubic ft (·06m^3 to ·08m^3) of plaster. Lime plaster had certain disadvantages: unless the sand used was sharp and completely free of salt, then white blotches might appear when the plaster dried and the mortar was liable to retain the moisture. For this reason plasterers liked working in a warm room and their bills often included charges for coal and peat.

In the latter part of the eighteenth century, a number of different plasters were developed and put into use, including a stucco patented by Robert and James Adam, who used their product for panels, bas-reliefs, festoons, griffins and mask-heads – all of the plaster embellishments used in their own architectural designs.

The country's heritage of ornate plaster-work can be seen in numerous castles, palaces and country and town houses. It varies in design, ranging from the elaborate plaster-work surrounding Jacob de Wit's Apotheosis of Hercules in the ceiling of Charles II's State Bedroom at Holyroodhouse in Edinburgh – dating from the seventeenth century – to the simpler, more classical lines found in the restored ceiling of the saloon in Culzean Castle in Ayrshire, originally designed by Robert Adam. Many less grand houses built by Georgian and Victorian architects also had ornamental plaster-work in their main rooms,

Opposite: St Paul's Cathedral, Dundee is just one of many conservation projects undertaken by carver Ian Ketchin.

(Della Matheson)

and it is the inhabitants of these houses today who are most likely to seek out the services of the ornamental plasterer. Bits of broken moulding and cornices are easily copied for repair work, and rooms that have been entirely stripped of their overhead decoration can be easily restored with pre-cast plaster detail. It is still possible to opt for genuine plaster ornament instead of the plastic substitutes that have appeared on the home decorating market.

The ornamental plasterers of today have a distinct advantage over their predecessors in centuries past. As Les Bickerstaff points out: 'Fibreglass and silicon moulds can be used again and again unlike the gelatin moulds which plasterers once used.' Bickerstaff, who served his time in Ulster, bought out the Edinburgh firm once owned by the late Albert Cramb. Cramb, a well-known city craftsman who did a lot of plaster-work at the Palace of Holyroodhouse was in business for 50 years and his many moulds passed to Mr Bickerstaff with the business. The moulding itself has changed little in process – liquid plaster is poured into a mould, allowed to partially set and then, if necessary, stabilised with the

Opposite page and left: fibreglass and silicon have replaced materials used in traditional moulds, but the process of making ornamental plaster, is followed in time-honoured tradition by Les Bickerstaff.

(Michael Siebert)

Below: drawing of wrought iron fence by Bob Hutchison.

addition of wooden rods (for lengths of moulding) or fibreglass. Animal hair is one ingredient that has become redundant.

Blacksmithing

'You used to be able to travel for five miles in any direction and find a village blacksmith', says Bob Hutchison of Kippin Smiddy. 'Most, of course, were tied to an estate.' Hutchison works in a kind of time warp – a picturesque old village smithy, owned by the National Trust for Scotland, west of Stirling. His work is far removed from the traditional smithing once carried on in this particular forge, but memories of the late Andrew Rennie, his predecessor, still linger. 'He was only 5ft tall but he could still swing a 14lb (6·35kg) hammer at the age of 94.'

Rennie, says Hutchison, was very much in the old tradition of the village smith. He was a sixth-generation smith and his forge was the hub of village life and information: people dropped in to hear the latest news and to reminisce.

The story of the transition of Kippin Smiddy from rural to architectural smithing illustrates the general shift in use of iron-working skills. Rennie, whose skill lay in shoeing horses and putting rings on wheels, had been driven more into architectural work before he retired, because as Hutchison points out, 'the carriage trade stopped.' Shoeing is a mystery to Hutchison: 'I could make a horseshoe, but I couldn't put one on with any confidence.'

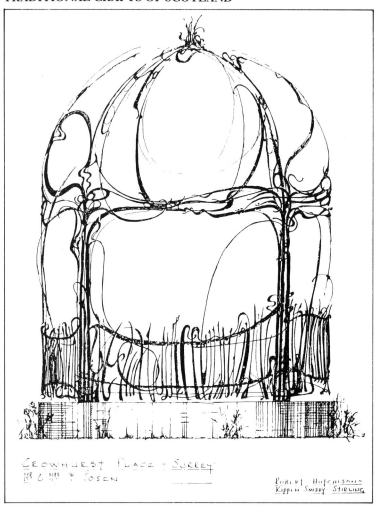

CROWHURST PLACE - SURREY
MR & MRS F POSEN

ROBERT HUTCHISON
KIPPIN SMIDDY STIRLING

Hutchison trained as a silversmith but never worked as a jeweller, and he arrived at Kippin Smiddy by a circuitous route. He worked as an estimator for Kingston Brass Company in Glasgow, and in the drawing office of Charles Henshaw's foundry in Edinburgh. It was the latter job which perhaps gave him the best grounding for, as he readily admits, 'no-one ever taught me blacksmithing.' And, indeed, when he took on Kippin Smiddy in 1983, he found himself in the slightly disconcerting position of having Rennie looking over his shoulder. The retired smith, who had the life tenancy of the flat over the forge, kept coming down the stair 'and hounding me like an apprentice', says Hutchison.

> Andrew didn't approve of what I made and I finally had to take a stand and assert my rights. I had to find my feet and I did – with a commission for General Accident in Perth . . . a 7ft [2·134m] high coat of arms in brass. Andrew couldn't work in brass, and when he saw what I had done he developed a grudging admiration for my work.

One of the most challenging pieces of ironwork made by Hutchison in Kippin Smiddy is a rotunda complete with furniture – a commission for a private client in Surrey in England. 'A lot of what I make is really enlarged pieces of jewellery', says Hutchison. The rotunda is perhaps a good example of this personal assessment of his work, for despite its iron construction, it has a light feel. It is 14ft

Above: garden rotunda designed by Bob Hutchison for Surrey client.

Right: the present occupant of Kippin Smiddy working at his forge.

(Michael Siebert)

Left: Hutchison likens much of his own work to 'enlarged pieces of jewellery'.
(Michael Siebert)

Below: the cast-iron railings of Edinburgh's New Town enhance the Georgian architecture.
(City of Edinburgh District Council)

(4·267m) high and 12ft (3·658m) in diameter and since its measurements far exceed those of the smithy, it had to be assembled in Hutchison's garden to make certain the parts fitted.

Denys Mitchell of Ragged School Forge in Kelso is another blacksmith who came to the craft in a roundabout way, though having decided what he wanted to accomplish he undertook training in smithing at West Dean College, Chichester, West Sussex. His work is executed on a sturdy scale, and the design is greatly influenced by the shapes of old weapons like battle-axes and halberds.

Mitchell has made a number of railings and gates, both for local houses in Kelso and for clients like the Standard Life Assurance Company in Edinburgh. Another type of architectural ironwork – cast-iron – can be found in many old properties, and it, too, requires the expertise of specialists, especially in conservation work. The many railings, gates, balconies, chimney-pots and street-lamps which are considered an important asset in Edinburgh's New Town, were originally made by casting, and replacement of these items today is usually handled by Charles Laing and Sons Ltd, the only foundry left in Edinburgh specialising in ornamental work. Like smithing, the work of this particular trade has also changed in direction. As Charles Laing says

Forty years ago when I started to serve my time our work was mainly in engineering. We cast work for trawlers – iron fire-bars for the engine-room, bronze valves and

T-pieces and bends in gunmetal. During the war of course it was Ministry of Defence work.

In the old days the ruling fact was the cost of the metal. Between 1920 and 1940 gunmetal was sold at sixpence a pound – now it is £2.30. Today the ruling factor is the men's time.

Laing's is a family business which was established in 1920, and it follows traditional methods for ornamental casting. Replacement work is undertaken by impressing a railing spoke or other pattern object into 'green' sand, i.e. sand which has been dampened. The molten iron is then poured directly into the mould. Laing's have made possible the replacement of innumerable New Town railings by this traditional method and have also provided the required decorative ironwork for other conservation projects, like the replacement of handles on stair-rails and fire-baskets at Holyrood Palace.

Stained Glass

The greatest success story in architectural crafts is to be found in stained glass – the medium which has found more supportive commissions in Scotland in recent years than any other decorative craft used in building. The Church of Scotland in particular has backed the work of the country's leading stained glass artists – especially through their Committee on Artistic Matters, which advises individual parishes about sympathetic and aesthetic alterations and additions to churches. The Committee's remit covers a broad spectrum of the crafts and includes tapestries, crosses and memorials, the provision of church furnishings and even colour schemes. These areas provide work for specialists in metal-work, calligraphy, wood-carving, and embroidery. As might be expected, however, it is the work of the stained glass artist which is used most frequently: the majority of consultations and discussions undertaken by the Committee concern this one medium, either in the realm of restoration or new commissions.

The renewed interest in stained glass is not confined to the Church: both the public and the commercial sector are making more use of stained glass. As a result, artists in stained glass are being given ever greater opportunities to create and develop non-religious themes – to use their skills as contemporary or historic muralists, or in partnership with interior designers and architects who can envisage modern applications of this traditional art form in terms of message, pattern and colour.

The oldest surviving examples of Scottish stained glass are the heraldic panels of 1542 in the Magdalen Chapel in Edinburgh. However, the bulk of our knowledge about Scotland's stained glass artists and heritage dates from the 1840s. It is believed that there was wide use of stained glass in Scotland in medieval times but only fragments of glass from this era have survived the Wars of Independence, the Reformation and changing fashion. The closure of churches, both this century and last, has also led to the destruction of many fine examples of glass. By a conservative estimate, Glasgow alone has lost over 300 of its churches since 1900.[3]

Several early nineteenth-century glaziers have a notable place in the development of stained glass in Scotland. The firm of Ballantine & Allan, founded in Edinburgh in 1837 (James Ballantine designed the windows in the Scott Monument and many in St Giles' Cathedral), was influential in the training of glass artists. David Kier of Glasgow became master glazier to Glasgow Cathedral in 1856, and with his sons installed the 60 windows designed by Max Ainmuller and made in the Royal Bavarian Manufactory. 'Munich glass' is now recognised as a bad episode in the history of Scottish stained glass and it is perhaps poetic justice that the windows succumbed to Glasgow's air pollution: commercial expediency in the techniques used by the Germans led to a quick deterioration of the enamelled areas of the glass. Much of the stained glass work made during this era in Scotland was in the Gothic style, then enjoying a revival in England and the output of Scottish artists of that time was greatly overshadowed by the stained glass creations made in the south.

Scotland's own distinctive contribution in stained glass is generally considered to have started in the person of Daniel Cottier, who practised his art in both Glasgow and Edinburgh. Cottier's work showed a number of influences: initially he was apprenticed to David Kier but he also worked and studied in London, where he derived a certain amount of inspiration from the lectures on decorative art given by John Ruskin, Daniel Rossetti and Ford Madox Brown at the Working Men's College. Cottier favoured strong primary colours and early in his working career, in 1865, he attracted much comment with the bold and original Egyptian motifs he used in the parish church in Townhead near Aberdeen. In fol-

Memorial window made by Douglas Hogg for St Andrews Church, Dundee. Detail shows glass painting technique.

(Douglas Hogg)

lowing years many others made their impact on the glass medium in the west of Scotland – the Glasgow studios of J. and W. Guthrie, which in the late nineteenth century employed well-known painters as freelance designers; the many artists who fell under the spell of Fra Newbery at Glasgow School of Art, and so on. There was tremendous activity in all branches of the decorative arts in the late nineteenth and early twentieth centuries and stained glass benefited as a result.

The reputation of Scotland's stained glass artists grew outside Scotland also – especially with the work of Douglas Strachan, an Aberdeen artist who studied painting in many different countries and who in 1913 completed a group of windows for the Palace of Peace at the Hague in the Netherlands. Strachan considered his finest work to be a window in St Paul's Cathedral in London, made for the Goldsmiths' Company in 1932 and subsequently destroyed during the London blitz. He also created seven windows for the shrine of the Scottish National War Memorial in Edinburgh Castle and innumerable other ecclesiastical commissions

throughout Scotland. Most of his work was unsigned and he left few workshop records, but attempts to record his work prove the breadth of his endeavour.[4] Strachan's career coincided with what is often referred to as Scotland's renaissance in stained glass and his work has been compared to some of the great windows seen at cathedrals like Chartres in France, Canterbury and York in England. More important, perhaps, was his legacy as an influence on the stained glass artists who followed. For two years – from 1909 to 1911 – he was head of the craft section at Edinburgh College of Art, where he initiated a lively tradition that has lasted to the present day. Edinburgh still has the only degree course in stained glass in the U.K.

The present head of stained glass at Edinburgh College of Art, Douglas Hogg, finds the purity of colour and the delight of working with light and colour one of the main attractions of working with glass – that and 'the ability of manipulating areas of colour where necessary.' Content is one of his earliest considerations in any commission but he is primarily concerned with the glass itself:

Painting on glass is, for me, a self-indulgence: coupled with degrees of etching and staining, one is in complete control of the elements of colour, light and form, of accenting and subduing. Perhaps because of this I regard stained glass as being separate from leaded glass, although both contribute equally as a decorative element in architecture generally.

Douglas Hogg has completed commissions for such diverse buildings as Culross Abbey in Fife and the Royal Scots Garrison Chapel in Werl, West Germany, a commission conceived as a demonstration and carried out with students at Edinburgh College of Art. A pair of windows given by the Boys' Brigade to Blackburn Church in West Lothian, made by Hogg, demonstrate the opportunities for interpretation available to present-day stained glass artists: one window deals with the aspect of preparing youth for manhood, which is, in turn, equated with spring. Evolution is recorded with a dragonfly next to a grub and a dove overhead. The Brigade's motto, 'Sure and Stedfast' infers, in the artist's mind, a darker and more sinister side which must be kept at bay, and he portrays this with a serpent contained in a yellow-stained cube under constant siege by light.

John Clark of Glasgow, who studied painting at the Glasgow School of Art, fell under the 'seductive spell' of glass while still a student. From the very beginning he liked the linear quality of the material and he liked cutting glass. At first he stuck to working with pure coloured glass and lines, but now he utilises the many different techniques available to the stained glass artist, including painting and staining. John Clark's first major commission – received while he was still a student – was to design a panel, 'Bird in Flight' for the natural history court of Kelvingrove Museum in Glasgow.

In a series of eight windows for the municipal buildings in Coatbridge near Glasgow he has taken the cubist approach to depict the industrial history of Coatbridge and its associations with mining, weaving, iron and steam engines.

John Clark begins each stained glass commission with a drawing. 'The composition and design are everything' he says. 'Churches are tricky because of their long vertical spaces.

The light box plays an important role in John Clark's development of a window.

(Glyn Satterley)

The suspended ceiling by John Clark, in Glasgow's new Princes Square development, gives the illusion of a glass-house dome.

(John Clark)

You can create space with glass but it need not be perspective space.' Following completion of his model drawing, he scales the drawing up to size, makes a tracing and begins cutting the pieces of glass.

In order to monitor the progression of the window as it takes form, he uses a vertical glass easel lit from behind to a strength of half daylight. Each piece of glass becomes an independent piece of the work and, depending on the technique required, could be either painted or etched, or both in combination. Painting and staining require firing, sometimes two or three times, and as each piece is finished it is stuck to the easel.

John Clark finds satisfaction in the fact that the technique he uses is basically the same as that followed by stained glass artists since the fourteenth century. Artists then would not have had the advantage of artificial lighting for their easels and the cutting tools may have changed somewhat (at one time glass was cut with a hot iron), but the piecing of coloured glass shapes with lead is a lingering tradition. The use of the lighted easel allows for adjustment before soldering. Individual pieces can be refired or repainted and the colour changed if they appear to be unworkable. Assembling a window is done on a flat surface, the pieces being soldered on one side and then turned and soldered on the other. 'In medieval times,' says John Clark, 'there was more of a division of labour in stained glass. You had designers and you had technicians. Artists, nowadays, tend to take windows through all the stages themselves, starting with the blank sheet of paper and ending with the installation.' It is a sobering thought, especially when the commission is large. One of John Clark's most recent projects was the creation of a suspended ceiling for a restaurant in the new Princes Square development in Glasgow. Creating the optical illusion of a dome reminiscent of a botanical glass-house – complete with ferns and leaves and parrots – was an imaginative and modern application of a centuries-old technique and the very positive employment of the craftsman in architecture.

1. Robert MacLeod, *Charles Rennie Mackintosh*, Middlesex, 1968, p. 56.
2. Geoffrey Beard, *Decorative Plasterwork in Great Britain*, London, 1975, p. 10.
3. Michael Donnelly, *Glasgow Stained Glass*, Glasgow, 1981, p. 5.
4. A. C. Russell, *Stained Glass Windows of Douglas Strachan*, 1972.

Select Bibliography

Adam, Frank, *Clans, Septs and Regiments of the Scottish Highlands*, Johnston & Bacon, Edinburgh, 1908 (reprinted 1970).

Beard, Geoffrey, *Decorative Plasterwork in Great Britain*, Phaidon, London, 1975.

Bennett, Helen, *Scottish Knitting*, Shire, Aylesbury, Bucks, 1986.

Capital Golf, City of Edinburgh, 1986.

Collinson, Francis, *The Bagpipe, the history of a musical instrument*, Routledge, Kegan Paul, London, 1975.

Collinson, Francis, *The Traditional and National Music of Scotland*, Routledge, Kegan Paul, London, 1966.

Cowen, Painton, *A Guide to Stained Glass in Britain*, Michael Joseph, London, 1985.

Cruickshank, Graeme, *Scottish Pottery*, Shire, Aylesbury, Bucks, 1987.

Dalgleish, George and Maxwell, Stuart, *The Lovable Craft 1687–1987*, Exhibition Catalogue, National Museum of Scotland/Incorporation of Goldsmiths of the City of Edinburgh, 1987.

Davey, A. et al, *The Care and Conservation of Georgian Houses*, Architectural Press, London, 1986.

Davie, Cedric Thorpe, *Scotland's Music*, William Blackwood, Edinburgh, 1980.

Donnelly, Michael, *Glasgow Stained Glass*, Glasgow Museums and Art Galleries, 1981.

Dunbar, John G., *The Architecture of Scotland*, Batsford, London, 1966.

Dunbar, John G., *The Stirling Heads*, HMSO, Edinburgh, 1975.

Farmer, Henry George, *Music in Medieval Scotland*, William Reeves, London, n.d.

Farmer, Henry George, *History of Music in Scotland*, Hutchison, London.

Finlay, Ian, *Scottish Crafts*, George G. Harrap & Co, London, 1948.

Firth, John, *Reminiscences of an Orkney Parish*, Stromness, W. R. Rendall, 1974.

Fleming, J. Arnold, *Scottish Pottery*, E. P. Publishing, London, 1973.

Fraser, Jean, *Traditional Scottish Dyes*, Canongate, Edinburgh, 1983.

Grant, I. F., *Highland Folk Ways*, Routledge, Kegan Paul, London, 1961.

Grierson, Su, *Whorl and Wheel*, Grierson, Perth, 1985.

Henderson, Ian T., and Stirk, David I., *The Compleat Golfer*, Victor Gollancz, London, 1985.

Kerr, John, *The History of Curling*, David Douglas, Edinburgh, 1890.

Honeyman, William C., *Scottish Violin Makers, Past & Present*, Dundee, 1890.

Kilby, Kenneth, *The Cooper and His Trade*, A & C Black, London, 1971.

Leach, Henry (ed.), *Great Golfers in the Making*, Methuen & Co., London, 1907.

MacCormick, Donald, *Hebridean Folksongs – A Collection of Waulking Songs*, ed. J. L. Campbell, Oxford University Press, Oxford, 1969.

Mackay, James A., *Rural Crafts in Scotland*, Robert Hale, London, 1976.

MacLeod, Robert, *Charles Rennie Mackintosh*, Country Life Books, Hamlyn Publishing, Feltham, Middlesex, 1968.

Manners, John, *Crafts of the Highlands and Islands*, David & Charles, Newton Abbot, 1978.

Moore, Jackie, *Rich & Rare – The Story of Dawson International*, Henry Melland, London, 1986.

Munro, Henrietta and Compton, Rae, *They Lived by the Sea*, Thurso, 1983.

Murdoch, A. G., *The Fiddle in Scotland*, 1888.

Murray, W. H., *The Curling Companion*, Richard Drew, Glasgow, 1981.

Reader's Digest Association, *Traditional Crafts in Britain*, London, 1982.

Robertson, James K., *St Andrews, Home of Golf*, MacDonald, Edinburgh, 1984.

Shaw, Margaret Fay, *Folk Songs and Folk Lore of South Uist*, Aberdeen University Press, 1986.

Russell, A. C., *Stained Glass Windows of Douglas Strachan*, 1972.

Savage, Peter, *Lorimer & the Edinburgh Crafts Designers*, Paul Harris, Edinburgh, 1980.

Smith, John, *Old Scottish Clockmakers from 1453 to 1850*, E. P. Publishing, Wakefield, 1975.

Wintersgill, Donald, *Scottish Antiques*, Johnston & Bacon, Edinburgh, 1977.

List of Addresses

It is not possible to list the many craftsmen and women in this book, but the addresses given here may be of use to readers wishing to inquire about the products or skills featured.

The two main administrative bodies for the crafts in Scotland are the Scottish Development Agency and Craftpoint. Both hold information about craftsmen and their work.

Crafts Section – Scottish Development Agency
Rosebery House, Haymarket Terrace, Edinburgh EH12 5EZ *tel* 031 337 9595.

Craftpoint
Beauly, Inverness-shire IV4 7EH *tel* 0463 782578.

Scottish Crafts Centre
Acheson House, 140 Canongate, Edinburgh *tel* 031 556 8136/7370.

Scottish Potters Association
c/o Auchreoch, Balmaclellan, Kirkudbrightshire *tel* 06442 205.

Scottish Glass Society
c/o Art Gallery and Museum, Kelvingrove, Glasgow G3 8AG *tel* 041 357 3929.

Scottish Crookmakers Association
9 Cauldside, Canonbie, Dumfriesshire *tel* 05415 297.

Scottish Association of Watchmakers and Jewellers
c/o 3 Silk Street, Paisley PA1 1HQ *tel* 041 889 3221.

North of Scotland Handloom Weavers Association
c/o 4 Station Row, Lhanbryde, Elgin, Morayshire *tel* 0343 842547.

Shetland Knitwear Trades Association
175a Commercial Street, Lerwick, Shetland *tel* 0595 5631.

Hebridean Knitters Association
7 James Street, Stornoway, Isle of Lewis *tel* 0851 3773 ex. 425.

Co-Chomunn Eirisgeidh Ltd
Community Hall, Eriskay, South Uist *tel* 08786 236.

The Harris Tweed Association Ltd
Ballantyne House, 84 Academy House, Inverness IV1 1LU *tel* 0463 231270.

Textile Workshop and Gallery
Gladstone's Land, Lawnmarket, Edinburgh *tel* 031 225 4570.

Dry Stone Walling Association
Young Farmers Club, National Agricultural Centre, Stonelea Park, Kenilworth *tel* 0203 56131.

Association of Weavers Spinners and Dyers
3 Gillsland Road, Edinburgh EH10 5BW *tel* 031 337 3984.

Index

(numbers in italics refer to illustrations)